We Who Gr

We Who Grieve

*Understanding Our
Most Painful Emotion*

RICHARD A. STACK

Jefferson, North Carolina

All photographs © Robert Denlow

ISBN (print) 978-1-4766-9283-8
ISBN (ebook) 978-1-4766-5054-8

LIBRARY OF CONGRESS AND BRITISH LIBRARY
CATALOGUING DATA ARE AVAILABLE

Library of Congress Control Number 2023050214

Front cover photograph © 2024 Shutterstock.
Back cover illustration by Beverly Ress.

Printed in the United States of America

Toplight is an imprint of McFarland & Company, Inc., Publishers

Box 611, Jefferson, North Carolina 28640
www.toplightbooks.com

To the kin who came before me
Upon whose shoulders I stand
Even those who never knew me
Yet have made me who I am

Table of Contents

Acknowledgments

If it takes a village to raise a child, a solid, supportive community is required to write a book. The following have helped shape my work in countless ways. I'll begin at the inception of the process.

While I mourned my mother in February 2010, Talya Husbands-Hankin handed me a book that inspired this project. Talya is the daughter of my cousin, Rabbi Yitzhak Husbands-Hankin. Yitz was my mother's favorite rabbi. I know the admiration was mutual. The book Talya gave me was Anita Diamant's *Saying Kaddish*, which comforted me by illuminating the rituals I was observing.

Working through my profound loss, I got the idea that a comparative study of mourning practices around the globe could be reassuring to others in the throes of acute grief. I shared this thought with Hilary Claggett, the acquisitions editor for two of my previous books. Hilary encouraged me to pursue this research.

Years passed. When the time came to transform the idea into a manuscript, unfortunately for me, Hilary had taken work with another publishing company. This one specialized in business books. Not the right fit for my project. But, helpful as always, Hilary forwarded resources that sharpened my proposal.

I am grateful to two graduate assistants who dove into the research of the mourning customs of various cultures. Julie Arthur and Adam O'Connor developed outstanding early drafts of the indigenous and Eastern religions passages, respectively. Bria Spivey bravely shared her lived experience mourning her murdered father. She also read and approved the pages on this painful topic.

Michael H. Rubin, the father of one of my favorite former students and a Louisiana lawyer who is a regional historian, was very

Acknowledgments

generous with his time. I thank him for explaining the nuances of the New Orleans jazz send-off, a most unusual funeral tradition.

I am indebted to the wonderful staff at the Wendt Center for Loss and Healing, a thought leader in grief and trauma counseling. For fear of omitting a name of any of the empathic case workers with whom I've volunteered, I will direct my appreciation to the executive director, Michelle Palmer. The training and small group experience afforded by the Wendt Center has brought to life my extensive literature review.

Tom Taylor, my dear friend and softball teammate of more than 40 years, has been a constant source of support. Tom wound down a career of community service as the bookstore manager of the Potter's House. The shelves of the bookstore featured works of social justice and spirituality. Tom's familiarity with specialty publishers led me to McFarland, where my latest work has found a home. Thank you, Tom, and go, you Mud Hens!

My friendship with Bob Denlow started in third grade and has never waned. He is the only person outside of my immediate family who has all four of my books and my documentary in his collection. That's loyal support. Bob has transitioned from a highly successful attorney to an avid photographer. His powerful photos grace several of my chapters.

Last—*and mostly*—I thank my beautiful wife, Beverly Ress. Not only is she the light of my life and my constant sounding board, but Bev is also a highly accomplished artist. Her colored pencil drawings are exquisite. Her creativity inspires me. Bev's work adorns the back cover of this book and enhances the experience of engaging with my written words.

Preface

The seeds of this book were planted when my mother died in the winter of 2010. As I was mourning this profound loss, sitting shiva in the Jewish tradition, I was handed a book written by Anita Diamant. *Saying Kaddish* explained the rituals I was observing in honor of my mother.

Kaddish is the prayer of mourning that curiously makes no mention of death or dying. Rather, it is an affirmation and appreciation of life.

I found Diamant's text enlightening. It clarified what was behind the customs I was carrying out. I began to see rituals as a crutch in the best sense of the word. When one has a broken leg, a crutch is a good thing, assisting the injured individual's mobility. Similarly, when one suffers a broken heart, a crutch helps him or her heal.

Reading the book gave me reassurance that I was not alone in my grief. In this I found comfort. It occurred to me that part of the healing process was establishing the contemplative space to think deeply about my lost loved one and my relationship to her.

As I gradually emerged from my grief, I became intrigued by how other religions dealt with death and comforted those left behind. When I shared my curiosity with others, I received a resonating response that let me know people were very interested in this topic. It struck such a chord that others offered anecdotes they experienced, opening windows onto different cultural perspectives.

At life's saddest moments, humans share the same emotions. We're all vulnerable and in need of support. Empathy is in short supply in our world and is never needed more than when one's heart is aching.

1

Preface

We Who Grieve: Understanding Our Most Painful Emotion is meant for those in the immediate throes of mourning. Clinically, this stage is termed "acute grief." Although there is no definitive time frame, this stage typically lasts three to six months but may extend much longer. The book also is intended for friends and family, those striving to be exquisite witnesses who are eager to support a grieving loved one.

In addition to exploring the mourning traditions of religions and cultures around the globe, this book encourages the bereaved to be patient and kind to themselves. It offers practical advice to the supporters of survivors as well.

This book has more than one objective. A main purpose is to provide comforting space for those who have lost a loved one, comforting space to contemplate and process their grief. The idea is that eventually that grief will be incorporated into a fuller, more meaningful life, one where a twinge of sadness comingles with hope to guide the future.

Another aim of this work is to assist those who are offering emotional support to mourners. Helping helpers do so in a kind, caring manner can go a long way toward facilitating grief.

The not so obvious intention of this text is to increase empathy in the world. With all the challenges that humankind faces—political polarization, poverty, climate destruction, disease, war, and all the other issues that tear us apart—there are a few universal forces that bind us. One is the overwhelming pain of losing a loved one. The births and deaths of the people we love stir the strongest emotions to which everyone can relate.

Love is at the core of grief. If everyone remembers that and offers the sympathy appreciated when they were in mourning, empathizes with the pain, and responds supportively, we will have come a long way toward the compassion necessary to change the world.

"'Tis a Fearful Thing"

by Yehuda HaLevi

'Tis a fearful thing
to love what death can touch.
A fearful thing
to love, to hope, to dream, to be—
to be,
And oh, to lose.
A thing for fools, this,
And a holy thing,
a holy thing
to love.
For your life has lived in me,
your laugh once lifted me,
your word was gift to me.
To remember this brings painful joy
'Tis a human thing, love,
a holy thing, to love
what death has touched.

Yehuda HaLevi (1075–1141) was a Spanish Jewish physician, poet, and philosopher, considered one of the greatest Hebrew poets, and celebrated for his religious and secular poems, many of which appear in present-day liturgy. His greatest philosophical work was *The Kuzari* (ca. 1140).

PART I

Meeting Grief Head-On

CHAPTER 1

Taking the Shovel

At my age, well into my 60s when these words are being written, I feel fortunate that I've experienced the losses of only three members of my immediate family. However, these deaths pierced my heart with near-paralyzing grief.

I've mourned the deaths of others, for sure, but only three have changed my life. They occurred in this order and at these points in time: my beloved grandmother, Rifka Hankin, my favorite person in my world, died when I was 29; my father whom I so admired, Norman Stack, died when I was 38; and I was 58 when my greatest teacher, my mother, Ida Stack, died.

A certain burial practice is the through line for these experiences, leading to the writing of this book. The evolution of my thinking about this custom made me realize the value of rituals even when we do not fully understand them. I wanted to dig deeper into cultures' (my own and others') methods for comforting mourners.

For those left behind, how is the excruciating pain of being a survivor eased? How does one get on with life?

In her profoundly personal reflections, Sherri Mandell examines those questions. She confesses that her broken heart will never be the same, that she will always long for her teenage son and feel the pain of his absence. But she believes it is possible to build a new heart.

"Many of us live with broken hearts," she writes. "But when you touch broken hearts together, a new heart emerges, one that is more open and compassionate, able to touch others, a heart that seeks God." Thus, Mandell explains "the blessing of a broken heart," the title of her tender narrative (Mandell, 7).

The burial practice I questioned takes place at the end of a gravesite ceremony. It is not unique to the Jewish faith, but this is how I've experienced it. As the prayers of mourning are concluded, the casket is lowered into the ground. Next to the burial plot is a large mound of earth, the earth that was displaced to dig the grave.

Mourners huddle together, moving the few steps from the makeshift tent where the prayers were recited to the pile of earth beside the hole. Two shovels have previously been jammed into the mound by groundskeepers. The shovels await the hands of community members who will start to bury the body.

The shovels are passed among the community participants. Each sorrowfully, dutifully drops a shovel's worth of earth into the hole, then gives the tool to the next person until it finally reaches the hands of family members.

When I was given the shovel at my grandmother's funeral, I thought, "How cruel. I'm actually expected to shovel dirt on my Bobbeh's coffin?" The action seemed disrespectful to the deceased. And it struck me as a harsh and hurtful gesture to her loved ones.

"How could you ask us to do this?" I thought. "Is this any way to show sympathy?"

It was a small Orthodox cemetery. No words were spoken. But it was clear what I was expected to do when the shovel came my way.

Later, when I asked about this custom, I was told simply that it is part of the finality of the funeral. It is meant to bring closure to the burial and begin the most intense phase of mourning, the one-week ritual of sitting shiva.

I found the brief explanation almost formulaic, not the least bit satisfying. My sadness was tinged with anger and confusion at not knowing why I just participated in shoveling earth onto the box containing my beautiful grandmother.

Nearly a decade later my dad died. When the shovel came my way this time, I knew what I was supposed to do. My attitude had softened from belligerence to acceptance.

I still wasn't crazy about the custom, but I'd learned that one way to interpret the communal shoveling is to think of it as the last favor you will ever do for the deceased, one he cannot return. I could see the sympathy if this is thought of as an act of mercy, a final kindness extended to one's loved one.

Twenty years passed, and it was my mom's time. She was a teacher of all things Jewish: Sunday school, Hebrew, Yiddish, music, theater, and bar and bat mitzvah training. At her frigid gravesite, the rabbi spoke directly to my brother and me.

"You may not know this teaching I'm about to tell, but your mother explained the custom in which we're about to engage this way." He was referring to the ritual shoveling of earth onto her casket.

"Your mother said that this final act was *like putting a blanket on a baby.*"

Like putting a blanket on a baby?! How could anyone object to that? In fact, who wouldn't want to participate in such a loving gesture?

With those few words, my mother had me doing a mental somer-

Hebrew headstone, Czech Republic, in small abandoned cemetery along a rural road south of Prague (2013).

9

sault, a feat of cerebral gymnastics that was nearly 30 years in the making. I had gone from bristling against this ritual to tolerating it and then embracing it.

As I stood over the gravesite and tossed a couple of extra shovelfuls of earth into the hole, I couldn't help but think, "Mom, you're teaching me still."

CHAPTER 2

A History
of Homeless Love

Grief is likely the oldest recorded human emotion. Findings of archaeologists suggest that the Neanderthals practiced ritual burial customs more than 60,000 years ago (Archer, 55). Since then, all human cultures have dealt with death in specific ways, signifying that human remains are not thought of as inanimate objects to be discarded. Rather, a corpse is considered an individual worthy of a degree of dignity.

Philosophers have pegged the origins of human society to when death was marked symbolically. Such markers might be considered "statutes" in the broadest sense. Human cultures have long invested resources in graves and monuments to the dead. Denmark, for instance, has more than 25,000 preserved burial mounds from the Stone, Bronze, and Iron ages (Brinkmann, 176).

Elsewhere, mausoleums and pyramids are paramount focal points for entire civilizations' social and economic life. Such material evidence of death's anthropological importance indirectly describes grief.

Grief is an individual's psychological connection with the dead. Memorials are society's collective bonds. There is no distinct line dividing the individual and the collective. A modest headstone serves as a material marker of the deceased's life and death.

While the main function of burial mounds and pyramids was to protect the dead in the afterlife, the memorials of secular societies are there primarily to assist mourners in coping with their grief. Both are a means of integrating the dead into the lives of their survivors.

Statues of children in cribs, Bellefontaine Cemetery, St. Louis, Missouri (2020).

All societies have a need to establish forefathers and foremothers in order to bridge present and past. In this way, links are forged offering the living a sense of belonging and understanding. Grief provides the psychological depth to reenforce these links.

For better or for worse, genuine grief belongs to humans. For worse, because grief hurts. For better, because it is a meaningful pain, a sensation that informs our fundamental emotional relationships.

The pain of loss is an element of grief. It is love without a home (Brinkmann, 60). The pain has meaning because it reminds mourners of their continuing bonds with the deceased. Eliminating grief's pain, even if it were possible, would be to erase a basic aspect of human nature.

It is through grief that human beings maintain bonds with the deceased. An accepted maxim is that grief is the price paid for love. This is significant in understanding the human condition, that is, the human capacity to form lasting, committed interpersonal relationships.

In his master work *Phenomenology of Perception*, the French philosopher Maurice Merleau-Ponty quoted poet Antoine de Saint-Exupéry: "Man is but a network of relationships, and these alone matter to him" (Merleau-Ponty, 530). This network of relationships could be considered the interdependence of human existence.

Thomas Fuchs, professor of philosophy and psychology at the University of Heidelberg, notes that in ways unlike other psychic phenomenon, grief reveals humans' basic need of others. "This ... mutual overlap of selves may be regarded as the most essential presumption of grief... This renders me fundamentally vulnerable, for in losing the other, I lose my self" (Fuchs, 195).

Grief keeps love alive, when the object of that emotion has died, and is an appropriate, almost obligatory, response to death. There is a normative imperative to grieve. This may be true of other emotions but is especially so for grief, given its bridge between love and death.

Bonds forged with others are both a gift and a curse. As such, grief can last a lifetime. Such mournful melancholy seems at odds with a society otherwise preoccupied with youth, optimism, and happiness.

"Each moment is a miracle and an agony," writes Sherri Mandell, reflecting on the death of her 13-year-old son. "A miracle that the world exists in all its glory. An agony that this world is one of suffering." Mandell explains, "Jewish tradition says that each person is a world. I have lost a whole world" (Mandell, 23).

Grief is a process in which the bereaved must "relearn" the world (Attig, 341). Grief is about building a new system of possibilities, some of which maintain bonds with the deceased.

So, there is good reason to dwell on grief. It represents that which is deeply human. The task of the bereaved is not to break their bonds with the deceased and move on but instead to maintain those bonds and proceed through life together with their departed loved one. The deceased persist in the form of stories, memories, and objects that frame the relationship.

A mourner's love for the one lost may grow even deeper than before death. A relationship still exists, one with the deceased's soul. Survivors' love becomes selfless because they are the ones who keep giving.

Proceeding through life links past with future. How can grief be accounted for within an evolving framework? What is the adaptive value of bereavement's nonfunctional behavior? When grieving, a person typically stops engaging in normal daily activities. One's production diminishes, which seems to contradict evolutionary momentum.

Many grief scholars, who otherwise adhere to theories of evolutionary psychology, consider grief in terms of survival value. John Archer suggests that the evolutionary function of grief—perhaps the ultimate separation anxiety—is that it motivates the mourner to seek reunion with others (Archer, 55).

Sociologists underscore the social and cultural ramifications of grief. David Émile Durkheim, the seminal French sociologist, is recognized with Max Weber as the principal architects of modern social science. Durkheim believed that how the bereaved integrate the dead into their lives is central to how society perpetuates itself. If the dead are not integrated, society disconnects from its past and from itself.

Humans have constructed memorials, written testaments, built shrines and cemeteries, and collected memorabilia to integrate the deceased into the life of the living. All of this links past, present, and future. Grief has been described as a thread "that moves across societies, institutions, communities, and relationships," binding these connections over time (Granek, 275).

CHAPTER 3

When the Sad News Hits: Fight, Flight, or Freeze

The Head and the Heart React

When humans detect a perceived threat, a primordial part of the brain kicks in. The amygdala, also found in other mammals and reptiles, dates back millions of years (Bruce and Leary, 224). One of the amygdala's functions is initiating the fight-or-flight response to danger. Grief can feel like fear and panic, an anxiety bordering on madness. This reaction triggers survival behaviors. Stimulation to the amygdala can come from any of the senses. When the brain translates new input as a threat, the amygdala ignites fight-or-flight mode. But if the stimulus is life-threatening with no time to fight or run, the third option is to freeze.

To hear of the death of a loved one, what defense is there? There's nowhere to run and no one to fight. This news is unlike any other stimulus that sets off a flight, fight, or freeze reaction. It's not that the survivor's life is threatened. Rather, it is irreversibly altered. In the aftermath of death when the shock subsides, an unfamiliar new life slowly becomes familiar. In the gradual process of change that Sigmund Freud called "grief work," the bereaved becomes accustomed to new habits, people, and places. New routines must be mastered and navigated, all without the lost loved one.

Everything that used to involve the deceased is different. When revisited, these things become new experiences but lack excitement associated with the new. This grief-stricken newness can be disorienting, even painful.

15

In time, the new rhythms of life become routine. As unthinkable as this may have been, these changes evolve to become the new familiar.

The stark fact of death—a person is here one day and gone the next—seems simple. But for the bereft survivor, change accompanying death is profound. No matter the circumstances, whether death was anticipated or not, the brain struggles, resisting while processing the new reality.

The Body Responds

Death rips apart the survivor's world, forever altering the mourner's landscape. The grief-stricken stumble through an environment that has disappeared, one that has yet to be rebuilt.

The news affects every dimension of the survivor's life. The precious loved one is gone as is the loved one's physical attachment. Sorrow engulfs the body. Disoriented, the survivor struggles to regain a sense of balance.

Grief reveals the bereaved's love for the deceased and represents an acknowledgment of loss. Grief is not a mechanical, passive reaction but rather a responsive understanding of a relationship that has changed. This recognition is felt in and expressed by the body.

The grieving body experiences a breach from a significant social bond, as it has been severed from deep relations with a loved one. Bereavement disrupts mutual interaction and demands the creation of new habits.

This means that grief work is not simply about writing new meaningful life narratives. It also is about how mourners alter the way they comport themselves physically in a changed social environment.

Grief is more than the rupturing of an important, isolated social bond. The experience also is shared with others: family, friends, and colleagues. Although this aspect has often been overlooked in grief studies, there is widespread awareness of the role of social groups in affording emotional support.

There is a basic range of bodily grief expressions across cultures.

16

"Crying, fear and anger are so common as to be virtually ubiquitous and most cultures provide social sanction for the expression of these emotions in the funeral rites and customs of mourning which follow bereavement" (Parkes, Laungani, and Young, 5).

Expressions of grief are nearly universal. This explains why those in modern times can reenact ancient Greek tragedies and relate to the grief felt by the original characters.

Crying is common when people reach language's limits of expression. In such situations, crying may be the last line of communication. The crying mourner is the embodiment of grief. Sad, mournful weeping might be considered a way to comfort oneself.

To cry is to experience a temporary loss of self. Crying externalizes one's emotions. It is a way for adults to comfort themselves. Weeping adults often close down on themselves, enacting a self-embrace as they deter distress and stifle audible dimensions of their cries. Such physical expression has a self-consoling effect.

Without denying the first-person nature of emotions, it should be noted that grief can be shared with others. There is an element of "it takes one to know one" in the phenomenon of collective grief. This explains customs of communal grief as enacted by some cultures' professional mourners. The traditional keeners of Ireland are examples of such practitioners.

In many circumstances, people recognize the influence of others' presence on a given experience. Being inspired by a sunset or a concert is a situation in which the company of others may make a difference.

This holds true for emotions such as grief. Patterns of crying can differ depending on whether the mourner is alone or with others. Similarly, silence experienced in solitude is qualitatively different from shared silence. The former may go unnoticed, while silence shared with others can feel awkward or safe depending on circumstances.

Silence surrounding death often is considered a problematic aspect of contemporary Western grief cultures (Doka, 187). In a culture that generally emphasizes emotional and verbal expression, others' silence may be construed by the bereaved as hurtful.

Conversely, mourners may feel pressure to express grief in circumstances they find uncomfortable. Either way, the presence of others alters the experience and meaning of silence and grief.

The Lingering Sting of Separation

There is a shared body-memory molded by the mutual interactions of being together that bereavement bursts. Dyadic memory is the part of recollection two people share. It is embedded in daily routines. To live with others is to let them in. The interactors become part of one another.

Those who live together are carried forward in the physical habits of their survivors. The death of a close loved one can feel like an amputation of the mourner's body. This is not merely a short-lived emotional experience and may affect moods fundamentally by establishing a lasting sensation of loss and lack of the other person.

The traditional ceremonies observed after death—funereal, memorial, and religious ceremonies—offer the recently bereaved slight, short-term relief. Other functions, legal and financial, require attention too. These after-death responsibilities provide the survivor with a way to stay briefly connected.

When the formalities are finished, the survivor starts a life absent the loved one. Grief will become a constant companion. First comes the physical emptiness. The loved one is no longer available to embrace. Tears, which can flow at any moment, may transform into a listlessness that inundates body and spirit. Former pleasures are diminished. What used to delight the senses barely registers. This is the starting point when sorrow becomes a full-body experience.

Several studies suggest that grief-related neuroimmune interactions within the body may adversely affect the health of a survivor. This may be a significant reason why many bereaved experience physical illness in the months after death (Holinger, 128). The shock of grief and its stresses can weaken the immune system, temporarily overpowering the brain's protective functions.

Knowing the odds of becoming ill increase following a dear one's death, what can survivors do to fortify their immune systems to maintain good health? Ways to lessen grief's impact include expressing the full force and effect of sorrow, accepting that one's appetite and sleep patterns can be disrupted, and realizing that one's thinking is not the same as it used to be.

Understanding what's happening to one's body and remaining patient about how grief can be exhausting may ease the burden on the immune system and reduce stress. Research about stress's effect on the body expands understanding of how grief attacks one's health. The benefits of time-tested recommendations should be considered: exercise and sleep, a healthy diet, social contact, and enriching, enjoyable activities.

When the shock of death overtakes the survivor, somatic grief can affect the body in other ways. Grief may numb a person's sense of taste, interfering with the ability to appreciate flavor. The pleasure of eating is thus diminished. A grief-stricken survivor may experience physical symptoms like those endured by the deceased. This is known as a "facsimile illness" (Worden, 147).

To experience similar symptoms or similar ways of talking or walking is a way to identify—even unconsciously—with the deceased. The similarity in symptoms or mannerisms can be a reminder of the lost loved one. Although the bereaved no longer can hug, see, or hear their loved one, adopting similar characteristics forges a connection and extends attachment.

It can be difficult to disentangle symptoms that are part of such masked grief. There are hints. Getting ill around the time of an anniversary of death or another family milestone such as a birthday or wedding anniversary can indicate masked grief. The experience of something physically wrong such as a headache may become the mourner's primary focus. Instead of an emotional response, the concern is how uncomfortable or painful a part of the body has become. A physical illness or a string of ailments can become a cycle that extends for weeks, months, or even years.

When death destabilizes one's world, the survivor's bearings are thrown off kilter. In death's aftermath, grief finds a way to be experienced and expressed. If not permitted an emotional outlet, grief may seep into the body, manifesting as an ailment or illness. Grief's movement cannot be predicted. It will go wherever it can find an outlet. If grief cannot be expressed emotionally, it may penetrate the body for its expression.

CHAPTER 4

Vocabulary:
The Language of Grief

To facilitate communication, a commonly understood vocabulary is helpful. Let's start with the terms "grief," "bereavement," and "mourning."

Grief comes from the Middle English word "gref," which means "weight." According to the *American Heritage Dictionary*, grief is "intense mental anguish; deep remorse; acute sorrow." Farther into the definition is the phrase "to meet with disaster."

Prehistory ended as the ice sheets subsided, making way for agriculture. Civilization was starting, and with it, burial customs to honor and remember the dead gradually were glorified. Funeral ceremonies grew into elaborate rituals. Memorials incorporated stylized art and architecture. Despite how elaborate the practices, how grand the structures, and how precious the entombed art, grief was ever-present. Grief is a timeless and universal sorrow brought on by death.

Grief is a natural reaction to the loss of a significant person in one's life. It consists of intense, often conflicting feelings including sadness, anger, depression, helplessness, and guilt. Physical symptoms may be involved including exhaustion, insomnia, and lowered resistance to illness. Grief can affect a mourner's mind, emotions, and body. It is likely to impact the ways in which one deals with all aspects of daily living. A mourner may experience a gnawing emptiness inside, a disconnection from other people and activities that were once a source of pleasure. These responses are a normal part of the grieving process.

One way to think of grief is that it is the price we pay for loving another so dearly. While death for the dying terminates a life, death for the survivor starts a new life, one without the loved one.

What follows a death? In the immediate aftermath, the deceased's body requires preparation and care. Simultaneously, survivors are thrust into deep sorrow. Human cultures have evolved rituals to assist the bereaved and guide the lost loved one's body through this significant transition. The lifeless form is attended to in accordance with mortuary practices, which have their basis in ancient times. An orderly progression of funerary customs readies survivors for the final farewell. Religious or secular, these rituals define the last moments the living will be with their loved one, but not before hearts break.

Bereavement is the period after loss during which grief is experienced and mourning occurs. C.S. Lewis notes that bereavement is an integral, universal aspect of experiencing love. He explains that it is not the truncation of the process but instead is one of love's phases (Lewis, 51).

Sadness and tears are part of the healing process. They are not to be feared. Rather, they come with the memories, sweet and otherwise, of the deceased. It is good to bear in mind a teaching from the Jewish tradition found in the Song of Songs: "Love is stronger than death."

The dictionary defines mourning as "the actions or expressions of one who has suffered bereavement." The same source adds that "wearing clothes conventionally expressive of mourning, as a black tie or armband, or entirely black clothes. Abiding by appropriate conduct." The major distinction between these concepts, then, is that grief is what one feels, including disbelief, shock, denial, anger, and sadness. Grieving is the experience of internal thoughts and feelings about loss.

Mourning has to do with actions and the outward expressions of internal thoughts and feelings. Mourning promotes adaptation and healing. As the explanation suggests, wearing black clothing is one way to express oneself. Weeping, lashing out in anger or frustration, and even collapsing can be physical manifestations of mourning. Observing rituals postmortem is another set of actions that expresses one's sorrow.

Often grief is seen as some sort of malady. Therapist and author Megan Devine comments that grief frequently is misconstrued as "a terrifying, messy emotion that needs to be cleaned up" as soon as possible (Devine, xvii). While we typically associate grief with death, it can be triggered by any serious loss. Divorce, diagnosis of serious disease, and loss of employment all are sources of grief. Such situations cry out for a mournful response. An especially severe loss may require as much mourning as the death of a loved one. The motions of mourning may prove as beneficial in processing a significant setback as they do in coping with death.

Grief has power that should be acknowledged. As unwanted as it may be, grief has its own creative, transformative force. It is a deep disruption of the soul, demanding recognition that one cannot press on as before.

"Sometimes we are formed more by what we are missing than by what we are given," writes Sherri Mandell (Mandell, 169). "Our courage and our compassion are built from pain." To believe—"This, too, is for the good"—even regarding one's suffering "is a truer way to live." While acknowledging that the sensation can be overwhelming, Mandell cautions that "the pain can either push a person into a spiral of depression or be an impetus for growth." It depends on how the mourner manages it.

Some of grief's sting comes from the loss of familiar sources of meaning. The bereaved must reinvent themselves and imagine life differently. While trying to trudge forward, grief also binds one to the past. Grief has a way of making life whole even as it splits one's heart. Grief won't let the mourner forget what life used to be like. Grief makes one pay attention to what otherwise might be missed. When grieving, the mourner often sees what's in shadows, a darkness that makes one afraid and is a reminder the mourner too will die.

Grief has its own function and rhythm. Grief's pain may be so overwhelming that its upside is overlooked. The mourner wants to loosen grief's grip and may have expectations of how long pain will last. But grief likely has other ideas, hovering until its work is complete. That can be a very long time. Many psychologists agree that it is only when mourners face their pain that they can start the slow process of healing.

Genuine grief rarely leaves for good. Even when it seems to have vanished, grief may make an unexpected appearance at any time. To fulfill its function, grief must be accepted and assimilated. The mourner needs to feel grief as purely as possible. No rationalizations are necessary. The bereaved should acknowledge their sadness to those around them. There is no need to be embarrassed or to feel above the sorrow. The mourners need to let down their defenses and let the grief do what it does.

Megan Devine cautions that mourners do not need solutions. She suggests that mourners need someone to acknowledge and hold their grief, to hold their hands while they simply stand in horror, staring at the abyss that is their life. Devine insists that some things cannot be repaired. They can only be carried (Devine, 3).

With the passage of time, one can refine grief. A transformation occurs when one starts to express grief directly and relates the images arising from the experience. A colorful set of stories penetrates the depression.

Grief may lead one to recall uplifting times with the deceased. Grief may have lessons about how to be a good friend to others in their time of need. As the bereaved refine the raw emotion, they may find that their pain is enhancing their empathy and relational skills.

In dialogue with grief, one should pay attention to what this sensitive situation is asking of the mourner. Imagining the mindset of asking grief "What is it you want me to do?" may turn up surprising answers. This questioning has led some to start a foundation, plant a garden, or install a park bench. Such creativity and generosity stem directly from grief. Socially conscious action helps soften the pain, easing one toward closure. Grief can spark a plan, helping one surface from sorrow.

Eventually mourners will stop experiencing grief as something invading their personal space. They will no longer be uncomfortable with it. It will become integral to who they are, part of their personality. Grief's lessons will be absorbed. The deep insights that grieving offers can redeem the sense of loss that has been endured.

The bereaved may value friendships more. Mourners may have greater appreciation for objects and places in their life. What had been the weight of pain may transform into character upon which a better life is built.

When one incorporates grief into daily living, it can work for rather than against the mourner. One senses relief not by having grief vanish but instead by leveraging its uplifting aspects. Grief can be transformed from an overwhelming emotion to an inspiration for creative output. Certain emotions cast a spell over those they inhabit. Sadness can be paralyzing. But with energy, those emotions can be channeled into creative action. Passive victims can become triumphant actors.

Grief is related to two words: gravity and gravitas. In a Jewish home where the seven-day shiva period is observed, the deceased's immediate family members sit on stools with conspicuously shortened legs. The squatty furniture literally keeps mourners down to earth.

Grief tends to make one more tenderly human. It lends personal weight to the mourner. If one bears the grief of numerous losses, a sensitive thoughtfulness develops. Such personal growth can be considered gravitas, giving weight to one's work and substance to relationships.

One can harness grief's power by responding to it imaginatively. Artistic expressions, gardening, and offering prayers all can give voice to grief. They lend external form to emotions, making them less threatening. Conversing with loved ones can help mourners turn grief into focused awareness, clarifying what is important and how changes may be made.

That grief can be overwhelming might be interpreted by mourners as a sign that it is time to expand their heart, allowing for greater love and connection. Grief can be a gateway to a more soul-centered life. Grief can hollow one out, making space for deeper insight and greater vitality.

As a master instructor, grief teaches appreciation of good and bad. In Jewish thought, even the bad deserves blessing. "Just as one utters blessing over the bad, so should he utter blessing over the good" (Berachot, First Tractate of Seder Zeraim, 54a). Grief trans-ports its students beyond romanticism and negativity, teaching that life is a constant mix of the easy and the difficult, the happy and the sad. Grief demonstrates how to endure pain without losing pleasure and how to react to tragedy without giving up hope.

If the bereaved can live their daily existence with full appreci-ation for the bittersweet nature of work and family, they will find deeper satisfaction in all they do. There is no more thorough study of life's bittersweet than to experience genuine grief.

Grief compels mourners to mature into well-rounded individu-als. It is a rite of passage leading to being a better friend, life mate, or teacher. This pain stirs new dimensions of compassion and empathy. It is a profoundly unsettling yet wise guide that prepares one for full engagement with life.

CHAPTER 5

Discussing Grief

To put a name to a feeling, to give words to an otherwise overwhelming emotion, can tame the feeling's power. Being able to put one's sensations into words can reduce the uncomfortable intensity being felt. Identifying emotions that were only felt before being named alters brain activity. To name what had been unknown is key to knowledge. Naming and learning rip the mask off mystery, neutralizing the unknown.

I conjure the image of a cartoon character wracked with unfamiliar distress. Breaking his silence, he identifies his ailment. His thought bubble fills with words describing his anguish. He can see and demystify the problem. He punctures the thought bubble, allowing calm to return.

Using words to express one's feelings can regulate what's being experienced. This affects brain and body. Thoughts shift from fear of death and loneliness to planning what comes next, which slows the heart rate.

In the aftermath of a loved one's death, the bereaved must learn the vocabulary of grief. The effects of the death usually are the first things described in this new language: the loved one is gone, life with the deceased is done, and the individual the mourner was is no more. The heartache following death is nothing one can see or touch. There is no physical substance. Yet, the emotion felt by those who've lost a loved one is sometimes compared to lead. Mourners describe feeling weighted down. Their world, they say, has turned gray, a colorless landscape.

Grief has staying power, because no matter how the bereaved experiences it, it engulfs the mourner. The influence is all-encompassing, making the body and the heart hurt. Grief's characteristics are not gentle or sluggish. Grief is dynamic, sometimes marching to a slow, steady drumbeat, only to pick up the pace of its relentless advance.

Grief may emerge in one form and change unexpectedly to another. Whichever mode it takes and whatever its label—acute, chronic, ambiguous, or delayed—it impacts the entire self. Dismal emotions and depressing thoughts—internal feelings that become externalized—trace back to the loss of the loved one. As time passes, it seems that grief refuses to leave. Yet, the survivor maintains the capacity to change.

For grief to morph, it needs space to uncoil. When allowed to flow, leaden grief can be transformed into golden joy. But the alchemy starts with grief. Lead precedes gold, as if in a fairy tale. Knowledge is powerful. To learn and understand is the acquisition of knowledge. To make what is unknown known has great impact, as does naming the unnamed. This can liberate one from the mystery of what is forbidden. To name the unnamed is to gain control of an altered life.

The Metamorphosis of Mourning

Grief's internal impact is not visible. The bereaved may have no words for the way people and places are perceived without the loved one. In sorrow's early stages, language is inadequate. Survivors have difficulty expressing how heavy their heart is, how badly their body aches. The places in the survivor's heart and soul that once registered the loved one's touch are not responsive. The lost loved one is painfully absent.

Although the mourner may understand what is going on cognitively, it seems that what's missing refuses to be named. A common reaction is that little makes sense. Progress needs to be made on a dual track. The bereaved needs to do "grief work," as Freud and others have called it, and grief needs to do its own work. Both griever and grief must change.

When grief is allowed to run its course, it takes control and advances at its own pace. Grief calls the shots, with no map or predictable timetable. Sorrow metastasizes, its presence a leaden yoke. Then, without notice, the stranglehold that death has had on the bereaved eases. Barely noticeable, an opening develops. Initially, the opening is narrow. Slowly it broadens, allowing the emergence of warm, fond, and funny memories. In this way grief, permitted to meander, morphs.

Different behaviors, absent the loved one, are consciously repeated. Like baby steps, gradually these new efforts grow into familiar experiences. As life without the deceased is lived through grief's variations, an altering of attitudes is perceived. Tears diminish. Tentative smiles grow broader. The attention span lengthens, enabling the reading of more pages. This is the process of grief ebbing, done without conscious intent.

Eventually comes the recognition that life is being experienced without the deceased. Mourners understand that they won't be slighting their loved one if they feel pleasure again. They accept that it is okay to be happy. This is the subtle but sure sensation of grief melting. Despite occasional eruptions of intense sadness, more positive times are recalled and lived.

Although sorrow is the essence of grief, it can transform into a nobility. Grief as despair can be changed into joy when bittersweet memories surface. Grief enabled makes way for pleasure to return, experienced differently but authentically. The pain of grief endured, sadness is spread among other emotions, allowing the emergence of happier memories.

Sherri Mandell speaks to this when referencing Rabbi Nachman, a nineteenth-century rabbi from Ukraine. Rabbi Nachman believed that being joyous was an obligation. The rabbi also lost a child. "He understood that in being happy, we give ourselves strength" (Mandell, 43). "Rabbi Nachman says that it is a person's nature to be drawn into ... sadness. When we struggle to be joyous we affirm God's presence... , his essential goodness." Mandell adds that it is believed that the prophets had to be joyous to receive the word of God. "God dwells in joy."

The bereaved reach a point where they are enriched by grief as they gain awareness that death and joy can coexist. Many mourners, having seen grief run its course, are surprised by sorrow's release. When grief is respected, past joys begin to mingle in the memory of the bereaved.

Roger Rosenblatt wrote two memoirs after the death of his adult daughter. The first, *Making Toast*, describes the depth of his anger and illustrates the clinicians' caution that it is easier to be mad than sad. Mad cloaks sad, keeping grief hidden. In his second work, Rosenblatt comes to grips with grief. While acknowledging he never again will see his daughter, the author concludes, "Love conquers death." Since her passing, "I have been aware, every minute, of my love for her. She lives in my love" (Rosenblatt, *Making Toast*, 146).

Well-Intentioned Well Wishes May Not Be So Well Received

Creating a life absent the deceased entails many changes. The survivor must learn how to not only feel in new ways but also navigate replies to condolence givers. During the depth of grief's sorrow, hearing unwelcome words from others can be painful.

The "Just Get Over It" Phenomenon

Mourners who hear phrases such as "it's time to move on" and "get over it" are well within their rights to be annoyed, even angry. They might keep in mind the framework within which such admonitions are offered. Ours is a society that frowns on being unhappy. No one wants to see a friend or family member down and out. So, "just get over it" is a sort of cheerleading, misguided though it may be.

Those who are comforting a mourner should reenforce the inherent permission to feel sad or feel any other emotion that comes naturally. Acknowledging the context in which comments from well-meaning friends may miss the mark can help offset the sting of "just get over it." A supportive friend might ask—or the mourner might ask oneself—what is truly needed in this situation. The answer can counter "just get over it." Part of the answer may be found in the

LDR formula for categorizing friends. L stands for listening, D for doing, and R for relief or respite. Which of the bereaved's supporters is good at which of the comforting behaviors?

Everyone has friends who are good listeners and others who are not. When the situation calls for reflective discussion, the mourner should gravitate toward those who are good listeners. It could be counterproductive to hold sensitive conversations with poor listeners.

Other friends might excel at doing (grocery shopping, laundry, etc.) or at offering relief (going for walks, playing cards, etc.). Choosing the right supporter for the right task can go a long way toward mourners meeting their own needs (phone conversation with Megan Seymore, senior therapist, Wendt Center, Washington, D.C., October 3, 2022).

What Future?

Expressions, however well intentioned, telling mourners that they will get used to the emptiness of their loss are not what they want to hear. Every fiber of the bereaved protests words that are aimed at the future. For one in grief, there is no future. Hearing that "things will get better" stings because it feels like a betrayal. It is as though beginning to feel okay means that the deceased will be forgotten.

The novelist Chimamanda Ngozi Adichie, writing of her father's death and the void he left behind, acknowledged that one learns "how much grief is about language, the failure of language and the grasping for language" (Adichie, 3). In *Notes on Grief*, Adichie observes that all her friends' expressions of sympathy, well-intentioned attempts to soothe her pain, were inadequate. She found the common comfort "he is in a better place" to be an especially grating, presumptuous cliché that warranted the response "How would you know?"

When consolation is offered that her father lived a long life, Adichie recoils. "Age is irrelevant." It is "not how old he was but how loved." With fresh insight, the author admits that her own previous condolences have been lacking. "Find peace in your memories," she once advised. Now she knows that rather than bringing relief, memories can produce exquisite pain. And while she used to believe that grief was a celebration of love, she now finds that sentiment heartbreaking.

For anyone who has "lost a loved one," that euphemism can come across as counterproductive. Mourners know all too well what happened to the deceased. They may even feel compelled to transform their anger into guilt, obsessing over how they may have thwarted the inevitable.

In the custom of Adichie's Igbo people of Nigeria, death is linked to settling one's accounts. "Clearance" is the payment of all outstanding debt. Without repayments, funerals may be boycotted. The tradition indicates how communitarian the culture is. Adichie does not want to tend to such issues but will because they mattered to her father.

In community, the author finds solace. Upon the death of a loved one, unfamiliar people tell previously untold stories. In their death, loved ones become more than they were ever understood, more than can be recalled alone. Retelling of stories is another way that accounts are settled, a way in which the community repays the listener many times over.

The Life Force

There is no telling how long acute grief will last. Part of its tyranny is that it robs mourners of their ability to remember what matters most. But life presses the living to forge forward. In the broader scope of its meaning, "eros" signifies "the life force." Eros is life's urging one to continue living. What nongrievers find difficult to comprehend is that the mourner's world must now be lived without its dearest loved one. Only the bereaved will know when the sorrow has subsided.

When people encounter new situations, thoughts put into words can help figure things out. Names and definitions, sentences building into paragraphs, make clear what wasn't comprehended. Words—spoken, written, sung, or signed—can put things in order.

The struggle of the bereaved to make sense of and articulate the meaning of their loved one's death from their own living perspective is a vital element of grieving.

Death invites survivors into the unknown. This exploration offers the prospect of renewal. Such renewal emerges through the new language of grief. What to say and how and when to express it are part of the struggle that challenges the heart and brain of the bereaved.

Historical Context

The history of death is about managing the transition to an afterlife, however defined. The narrative switched from the medieval preoccupation with the soul's salvation to early modernity's concern for the corpse. Gradually, scientists were permitted to examine bodies after death. Early religious concerns regarding the destiny of the soul gave way to focusing on the fate of the bereaved. After all, it is the survivors who must carry on without their loved one.

This meant mourning observances that had been cultivated for how they served the deceased's soul being replaced by emphasis on how the grieving process assisted the bereaved's return to life in society. The mission of monuments and memorials shifted from ensuring the deceased's salvation to aiding the bereaved in their expression of grief.

In contemporary times, the focus continues to be on the bereaved. Grief customs no longer are primarily for the sake of the deceased—to ensure safe passage to the hereafter—but instead are for the benefit of the bereaved to secure a sound psychological journey through the remainder of their days. This holds more so for faiths that do not subscribe to a funerary theology that engages rituals to assist the dead on their way to heaven.

Modern society has transformed from a religious culture to a psychological one, from care for the deceased's soul to concern for the bereaved's psychological well-being. This perspective is consistent with the view that psychology has replaced religion for the individualized human. Psychologists are becoming more priestlike, dispensing advice, relieving symptoms, and aiding in the individual's growth.

For the British of the nineteenth century, the death of Prince Albert, Queen Victoria's husband, set the standard for mourning. The rituals of 1861 continued throughout the Victorian era, later coming to be seen as an obsession with death. Grief changed from a normal aspect of life, expressed through rituals and religious practices, to a defining emotion of the Victorian era, when it was refined in art and literature. Elaborate mourning practices emerged, independent of religious context.

This began to change again with the first major war of the twentieth century. From that point forward, grief became more concealed and constrained, eventually leading to medicalization. Grief now seems to have become a central phenomenon through which humans may be understood, especially by way of popular culture.

In America, things were different. The Civil War, with its overwhelming rate of death in the North and the South from 1861 to 1865, compelled significant changes in the expression of grief. Tallying deaths from both sides, approximately 750,000 people perished during the war. This amounted to roughly 2.5 percent of the country's population at the time.

Given both sides' staggering losses, it was not possible for Americans to grieve as they previously had. There was no longer time or money to mourn in customary ways. In conflicts that followed—World War I, World War II, the Korean War, and the Vietnam War—public grief continued to recede. By the 1920s, American grieving mostly went underground. For many, the tradition of wearing black was no longer observed, at least not for as long.

Following World War I, more subtle displays of grief were adopted to honor those lost in combat. One such symbol, the "remembrance poppy," was inspired by poetry. It is still used by many countries, with lapel pins bearing the poppies worn as visible reminders of loss.

In the twentieth century, bereavement in the United States grew more solitary. Devoting less time to mourn came to be considered

Autumn field of military markers, Jefferson Barracks, St. Louis, Missouri (2020).

reasonable. The trend continues. Grief has become not only private but also somewhat hidden. Little time is afforded for coping with loss. The expectation seems to be that one returns to work after taking a day off to mourn.

In the US youth-obsessed culture, it is bad enough to be old. It is nearly taboo to talk of death. Talking about death does not violate any norms; it is just rarely done. When a celebrity passes, the country pauses to honor the individual's career. Obituaries are moved to the front page. Online and broadcast remembrances dominate the short-term news cycle. When a prominent national figure dies, flags may be lowered to half-staff.

Collectively commemorating the loss of high-profile individuals is an exception to the typically tight-lipped approach to the subject. It seems natural for people not to like, witness, or talk about sadness. But grief is more than being sad. It is a yearning for the person who passed. It recognizes that survivors are no longer the people they were. It acknowledges a major absence from the mourner's life.

Due to reluctance to talk about death, such discussions can

draw us into a sacred space. Otherwise, opportunities to honor the moment may be missed. Such a situation occurs when the silence is breached during televised sporting events. The announcer may comment how courageous the young quarterback Smith is for taking the field the day his father died. Certainly it is a timely topic, as the athlete must contend with overwhelming emotions as he chooses to compete in the wake of heartbreak. Doing so merits mention as a factor influencing the performance of a key player. As an element of human interest, it elicits our sympathy. But to call it "courageous" may be missing the mark.

In Joan Didion's *The Year of Magical Thinking*, the author speaks to the roots of quarterback Smith's attitude (Didion, 60). Didion cites a series of lectures delivered by Philippe Ariès at Johns Hopkins in 1973. Ariès observed that a revolution took place around 1930 in the way Western countries viewed death. Ariès noted that death had been all too familiar and would become a shameful subject.

Didion referred to English social anthropologist Geoffrey Gorer, who accounted for the rejection of public mourning as a result of increasing pressure from a new ethical mandate to enjoy oneself. There emerged a duty to refrain from diminishing the enjoyment of others. That trend treated mourning as morbid self-indulgence. The bereaved who hid their grief stoically and completely were worthy of social admiration.

Not to be judgmental, but perhaps if our society were more sympathetic, the sporting public would understand that some athletes need to be alone with their emotions and with their families. The expectation would be that the process of personal healing takes priority over playing. Then, perhaps, quarterback Smith would have more viable options.

A notable exception to celebrity silence occurred during a CNN broadcast on August 15, 2019. Anchor Anderson Cooper interviewed Stephen Colbert, host of the CBS *Late Show*. The two exchanged worldviews, sharing experiences covering Donald Trump's presidency. Toward the end of the interview, the subject turned to grieving. Cooper was still processing his mother's death. Gloria Vanderbilt had died two months earlier at age 95. Together yet in separate spheres, mother and son had grieved the death of Anderson's father, Wyatt Cooper, in 1978. A decade later, Anderson's older brother, Carter, committed suicide.

Colbert, who speaks of his Catholic faith humbly and earnestly, had a childhood marked by tragedy, a 1974 plane crash that killed his father and two brothers. At the time, Colbert was 10, the youngest of 11 siblings. Responding to Cooper's interest in how those losses shaped him, Colbert said, "You become a different person.... You kind of re-form yourself in this quiet, grieving world."

Colbert explained the faith that sustained him. "If God is everywhere, and ... in everything, then the world ... is ... an expression of God and His love. You ... accept it with gratitude, because what is the option?"

Cooper then cited another interview of Colbert's in which the comedian said he had learned to "love the thing that I most wish had *not* happened.... What punishments of God are not gifts?" Colbert elaborated on the gift of loss. By knowing grief, he has grown into an adult who can understand it in others. "I want to be the most human I can be, and that involves acknowledging and ultimately being grateful for the things that I wish didn't happen, ... [because] they gave me a gift." Cooper added, "This is part of being alive.... Sadness, suffering.... You can't have happiness without having loss and suffering."

Colbert concluded the conversation by referring to his devotion. "In my tradition, that's the great gift of the sacrifice of Christ—is that God does it, too. That you're really not alone. God does it, too."

CHAPTER 6

Two Distinct Coping Styles

I've come to learn there are two basic styles of grieving: intuitive and instrumental. The intuitive mode is emotional. Individuals express outwardly what they are feeling inwardly. They need time to adjust gradually and share their feelings. Those who grieve instrumentally are stoic, keeping their pain and anxiety internal. Such people tackle the immediate tasks of funeral arrangements and memorial services. They cope by doing. This may be the coping style of the quarterback who decides to play in the aftermath of a loved one's death. Even so, game announcers' emphasis on the courage to play may be a disservice to the deep reflection that mourning deserves.

One must understand grief in order to deal with it. Most people lack education about grief. However, it is vital to get a handle on the basics of this powerful emotion to eventually free oneself from grief's grasp. Rationally, we all know we are going to die someday. Reminders surround us: cemeteries, obituaries, and mortuaries. When we're young, the death of a pet may give us our first sense of sadness and loss. Extrapolating from that experience, we know that death will come to our loved ones, and when it does it will hurt. We know too that ultimately we will succumb. Even with this awareness, we do not dwell on death. We are not preoccupied with our own demise, and nor, in a healthy frame of mind, should we be.

Rather, we march forward, making the most of life's opportunities while checking off milestones such as graduations, career launching, falling in love, getting married, starting a family, buying a home, filling it with stuff, and retiring. We do all this with little thought of our endgame.

In an instant, all our dreams can come crashing down. A tragic accident or deadly diagnosis can turn our world inside out. Our sense of well-being is destroyed. The safe, satisfied world we knew is no more, replaced by doubt and sadness. We become vulnerable in ways we could not have imagined. The pain of the moment can be overwhelming. Accompanying such grief can be a powerful explosion of emotion. Sadness sets the framework for our outlook. When a loved one dies, feelings never before experienced may surface in unexpected ways. These sensations are apt to get the best of us. One might wish not to confront them. One might prefer that these feelings be locked up and hidden. "Why don't these feelings leave me alone? When will they go away?"

Unfortunately, they will not. They are integral to the memory of loved ones. The excruciating pain experienced is the flip side of the love that was shared. Far better to deal with one's grief than to turn away from it. Grief is part of the spectrum of human emotions, not a feeling to be ignored. When the bereaved think that they would prefer to have grief fade away, what is meant is that they would like relief from their awful sense of loss. After all, what sort of human being would not grieve the passing of a loved one?

One reason why many mourners live so emotionally spent is that modern life does not allow the necessary time to confront grief. In other cultures, a typical mourning period may last a year or longer. In contemporary society, one in mourning may be given a day or two off from work and then be expected to put sorrow behind and move on. But as the bereaved return to daily routines, they are likely to feel a dull ache that won't let go. It is essential that mourners allow themselves the space, time, and energy to work through the dimensions of loss.

For a time, the mourner is suspended between grief and renewal. A pendulum swings between these extremes of existence. The darkness of loss gradually gives way to light and hope. After my father's death, with the steady guidance of my mother, she, my brother, and I observed the rituals of sitting shiva. "Shiva" is the Hebrew word for "seven." We said morning and evening prayers daily all week. Mirrors were covered. Appearances were subordinate to feelings. The rituals of vanity are a luxury to be ignored. A mourner wants to forget the material world and be transformed into a spirit that can merge with the deceased. The world is shadowy, the body insubstantial. When visitors came to pay their respects, my family was seated on foot stools, while our guests sat comfortably and noticeably higher than the mourners. The idea was for us to be literally lower to the ground. Being closer to the earth is a symbol of humility.

Most people find it hard to tolerate a mourner's silence. They rush to fill the void. Jewish mourning laws dictate otherwise. One paying a shiva visit is to be silent until the mourner speaks. If the mourner says nothing, the visitor also should remain quiet. Neither should greet the other. When the pain is most intense, during the first three days, it is said that the mourner is like a fragile egg, without a mouth, sitting in silence. The point of the shiva is not to comfort the bereaved but rather to be with them in their time of grief. The purpose of the shiva is to relieve the bereaved of their loneliness (Mandell, 53).

One expresses compassion for the mourner through silent presence, just as Job sat with his friends for seven days with no one uttering a word. It is believed that only God can comfort. This explains why many traditional Jews depart a shiva with these words: "May God comfort you among the mourners of Zion and Jerusalem."

What I most remember is that other than a Friday night trip to the synagogue, we didn't set foot outside the house for seven days. Our mutual misery supported and comforted each other. It was the dead of winter, and to be stuck inside by ritual seemed fitting. When the eighth day arrived and we walked down our street hand in hand in hand, it felt as though we were given permission to breathe again. With the fresh frozen air, our healing began.

More than any of nature's creatures, humans possess the capacity to remember and express what they are feeling in constructive ways. The ability to communicate powers us through the most difficult times. To express grief is the way to work through pain and gradually get our lives back on track. Suppressing grief derails the healing process.

CHAPTER 7

The Power of Prayer

Prayer is a concept so embedded in our language and culture that it is rarely examined. Not often do we pause to ask what it means. The definition a child might give, and it is as good as any, is that prayer is talking to God or perhaps asking something of God. Many people, whether believers or not, find themselves instinctively seeking help from a higher power when the need is urgent. It is a reaction to helplessness when conditions of sorrow are overwhelming. Death and bereavement certainly fit this category of human experience. The idea of talking to God opens a new way of seeing what is happening. Prayer invites the sufferer to rise above pain and view matters from an elevated perspective, similar to how a mountain climber looks back on the valley from heights scaled. A new vantage point offers a fresh look.

Mystics from all backgrounds have been imbued with awe and wonder as they fathom the presence of a life force. A function of the human condition is getting stuck in a myopic perspective. A narrow point of view can be limited by geography, ethnicity, culture, religion, and so on, all inhibiting imagination about what is not directly known. Although people struggle against these restraints, we tend to let our firsthand experiences, emotions, and concerns overtake our senses and allow worries to screen out everything else. The world's great religions, on the other hand, remind us that it is possible to gain release from narrow-minded perspectives. Religious traditions provide the stories, ceremonies, and Sabbaths needed to spark the inspiration to take in a much larger picture.

Praying, which may manifest as meditation or may take simpler forms of asking, offering thanks, or caring on behalf of others, is about shifting consciousness to gain new perspective. Being less pre-occupied with oneself, one is less apt to view others as competitors or rivals. Many religious outlooks suggest that we are one another, as was well put by the Anglican poet John Donne: "No man is an island." All humankind is connected. To harm another human being is bound to cause the perpetrator to suffer.

Praying for another means that the worshipper is involved with the well-being of the other. This links the health, happiness, and welfare of both parties. Religions encourage followers to transform prayer into action. Feeding the hungry, clothing the naked, and housing the homeless are such edicts.

With the environmental movement, many worshippers began praying for Earth and its inhabitants as well. The threat to the health and survival of the planet has become clearer. Tribal peoples have long had an awareness of the natural world's well-being, as their survival is intricately linked to the plants they harvest and the animals they hunt. More industrialized societies have awakened to the need to shepherd the environment even if the inhabitants of such cultures have not grown or gathered their own food for generations. Just as people need to be cherished, nourished and protected, so does the natural environment. Those in more "sophisticated" societies are painfully learning this. Having forsaken wonder in the face of nature, modern civilizations have exploited the planet, poisoning rivers, damaging habitats, and hunting animals into extinction. The recovery from this desperation is a fresh perspective, a collective denial of ego and greed that all faiths advocate.

So, in its essence, prayer is about gaining new perspective on the world or recovering earlier insight. It is about a rediscovery of wonderment and awe, of love and joy. Through a turning to one another and a deference to the natural world, prayer can transform the grief and pain of loss into wisdom, empathy, and appreciation.

Grieving Without Believing: An Atheist Perspective

An expression born from the horrors of war is that there are no atheists in foxholes. Research psychologists contend that religion is rooted in the fear of death. It also has been noted that many people become more religious as they age (Bengston, Putney, Silverstein, and Harris, 363). This trend could be attributed to religion's ability to give meaning to mortality. Some assume that confronting death without religion leaves life pointless, even unbearable. Only the exceptionally stoic can face death without the support of religion, the assumption goes. But there's little data to back this up. Few studies have focused on secularists who confront death absent religion.

This raises two questions: How do atheists and agnostics seek meaning at the end of life? And how do they order mortality without religion? On the surface, the foxhole theory seems to hold. Substantial research indicates that religion assists those coming to grips with dying (Bengston and Silverstein, 26). Some of that influence is connected to the community support offered by organized religion. Providing meaning is an important aspect as well. A sense of coherence can be found in religion, a confidence that life events are purposeful rather than random. This can bring a feeling of control over one's life (Wozniak, 259–68).

"Are you going to heaven?" Illinois State Fair, Springfield (2018).

Dying is scary because it is an unknown experience. No one knows where they are headed. Life's end stages may involve physical pain, the inability to partake in activities once taken for granted, or the loss of cognitive functioning. For many of the elderly, late life brings the loss of spouses, other family members, and close friends who may have been sources of support.

Religion can frame why one is in pain or why a loved one had to die. This is the case when suffering is considered redemptive or an element of divine design. Religion also offers answers to what transpires after death, whether through the Buddhist or Hindu conceptions of reincarnation or through the comforting reassurance of some Christian traditions that the deceased is in heaven and will be seen again.

Depression can increase among the elderly, especially for those caring for an ailing life partner or who lose their mate. Religious traditions can offer supportive networks. Rituals can provide guidance to process devastating losses and maintain a meaningful life. Meditating or studying scripture can be done, even by those with disabilities. When a loved one dies, customs such as sitting shiva and preparing for a funeral mass lend structure to survivors.

But believing that religion helps adherents find meaning when facing death is not the same as saying that there is no meaning without religion. Reviews of such research suggest that the focus is generally on religious individuals. The studies usually compare more devout people with those who are less so. Rarely do the studies emphasize those who are committed seculars, that is, people who have substituted religion with some other form of meaning (Hwang, Hammer, and Cragun, 608; Weber, Pargament, and Kunik, 72).

Those studies that do compare closely suggest that nonreligious people do just fine. Peter Wilkinson and Peter Coleman discovered that both atheism and religion can be a source of meaning for people facing death. What counts is the strength of conviction. It is that, not whether one is religious or nonreligious, that empowers effective coping (Wilkinson and Coleman, 337).

Other research suggests that although uncertainty can be associated with depression, questioning can spur growth. Bethany

Heywood and Jesse Bering have demonstrated that the nonreligious do frame life events using intentional narratives (Heywood and Bering, 183). Little is known about the content of these narratives. What is known is that seeking meaning is an interpretative behavior. Human beings make meaning by telling stories about their lives (Gockel, 189). Language both reflects and creates experience. Even when telling stories similar in content, people use linguistic, rhetorical, and structural devices to create different meanings.

Broader social narratives can shape individual storytelling. Such social narratives can stem from religion, science, family background, and popular culture. Meaning making can be thought of as a sort of mapmaking. The stories people tell are a way to connect the dots of their lives and orient themselves. It is similar to the ancient Greeks imagining lines between the stars to give the constellations their names. Absent a constellation map, events could feel random, and the storyteller could feel lost. This confusion intensifies when one is approaching new terrain.

A map provides a path to follow and offers agency for the traveler. Religion is recognized as a powerful mapmaking tool, as it creates meaning, and is full of generic narratives that operate as a cultural tool for constructing meaning. These narratives inform and frame each believer's personal story. An area to be explored is how this works for nonreligious people. Are there generic stories that secular adults use to make meaning, especially as death nears? If so, how do they rework these narratives to create meaning from their personal experience?

The nonreligious can be categorized in a number of ways. Atheist, agnostic, humanist, and freethinker are among the main classifications. Studying these types poses challenges. One is theoretical. This is a population defined by what they lack, namely religion. Yet, there is little agreement on what religion is. The models of religion familiar to the social sciences largely are based on Christian constructs.

Reputable polling firms employ measures such as belief in God, prayer, attendance at services, and denominational identification with specific traditions and then apply these cross-culturally to places such as Japan and China, even though this is a poor match. Even in the United States, where the dominant religion is Christianity, roughly half on the nonreligious claim their religion to be "nothing in particular." This identity leaves leeway for further definition.

Another challenge lies in the methodology of researching the nonreligious. How are they accessed? The ranks of the religious can be located through the organizations with which they affiliate. It isn't that easy with those who do not claim a religious association.

A sizable majority of self-identified atheists are not members of atheist organizations. The negative image associated with atheism in the United States complicates the issue (Edgell et al., 607). This is especially true for African Americans and the elderly atheists, for whom religious affiliation is still a strong norm. Thus, being openly involved with formal atheist groups could lead to being ostracized by the community.

There is likely selection bias involved. Respondents in an end-of-life survey may be quite comfortable discussing their thoughts on the topic. Meaning making is especially salient when people approach the end of life. Death is humanity's most profound crisis of meaning. Confronting mortality sparks an assessment of the days left behind and the ones still to come: good experiences and bad, what one's legacy may be, and whether there is time to improve it. Meaning making in the final stage of life looks both backward and forward, charting past and future.

Research confirms some of the assumptions about nonreligious people. Most of the nonreligious do not believe in an afterlife, not in the sense that a spirit or soul or some conscious aspect of self lives on after one's brain dies. The majority does not think that human life has an inherent purpose. Perhaps counterintuitively, this does not lead to despair. Instead, research reveals that secular seniors construct their own meaning-making narratives from secular sources as opposed to religious ones. There are patterns of secular meaning making comparable to those found in religion.

Certain types of stories recur indicating that these meaning maps are not idiosyncratic. Rather, they are emblematic of an ideal sort of narrative that the nonreligious use. Such narratives serve the same purpose as their religious counterparts by establishing coherence as they structure the past and by establishing control as they offer action steps moving forward. Similar to religious narratives, they suggest a moral dimension. They express a meaning to existence that is greater than the individual.

A common narrative framework is based in the scientific understanding that everyone is part of nature. Earlier studies suggest that scientists are more apt to be nonreligious than the general population (Ecklund and Lee, 728).

For doctors, engineers, and biologists, among others, science can function as a meaning-making narrative. Science is sometimes thought of as hard, cold, and value neutral. Yet, narratives ground in science can evoke awe and wonder. Science may produce a perception that everyone is part of a meaningful world that structures the past and provides insight for the future.

With some variation, the arc of the science narrative is that humans are part of nature and have a place in evolution and a role in the ecosystem. The human role is ever developing. What happens to individuals has material causes explained by science.

Although an inherent purpose in the universe may be lacking, humans can create meaning for themselves. Life is interdependent. Humans' actions ripple throughout all aspects of nature. Death is part of life, reminding humankind of its kinship to other animals. Yet, human intelligence also imposes a moral imperative to pursue understanding through science. This obligation extends to preserving the planet for future generations.

Charting the Past

Science narratives explain life in terms of material causes. Reflecting on their past, the science-oriented may speak of good or bad fortune, of random natural events, of winning or losing a social or genetic lottery that influences one's ability to make good or bad decisions. The science narrative holds that individuals do not control what happens to them. But they can control their reactions. Every choice made determines its consequences. There is no belief that any force is micromanaging anything. No one is to blame for any hardships experienced in life. All that befalls individuals is necessary for them to become who they are.

This perspective has an edge to it because nature is not fair. But there also exists a beauty in the randomness that evokes awe at the unexpected. The butterfly effect is in full force, that is, the belief that the flapping of a butterfly's wings in one part of the world can set off a tornado across the globe. This is a metaphor for both the muscle of tiny changes and the limits of human control.

Charting the Future

From the point of view of natural science, death is the end of an existence. Still, life goes on. In a way, the physical body is recycled and nourishes future plant life. A scientific account might add that as with anything on the planet that dies, a human's atoms and energy are reabsorbed into the universe.

For those who have children, their genes live on through them. Legacies are the impacts felt by others, through caring for friends or family or community.

A Moral Universe?

Atheists might be considered arrogant, since they do not recognize a higher power (Edgell et al., 607), but the opposite may be true. Seeing themselves as part of nature instead of created by God and in his image may draw the scientist into a deep humility. Nonscientists' prevailing view of science is that it is morality neutral. However, many who lean on the science narrative find it coupled with a moral obligation. The science narrative comes with a moral urgency to what adherents feel should be done with the time they have remaining: express love for their family and friends, appreciate nature and art, and be active politically even as they may grow increasingly physically disabled.

Many of the research findings point to the flaw of the foxhole theory that fear of death pushes people toward religion. Rather, awareness of death motivates a quest for meaning. Secular underpinnings such as science can be as rich a source of meaning making as religion is. Religion often is credited as the only way to address the fear of death. Perhaps it is merely the oldest and most popular way. It seems that generic secular narratives also work well to provide meaning when confronting death. Secular meaning-making maps bear similarities to religious ones: they establish coherence and control, position human experience in relation to something bigger than the individual, and furnish moral significance to lives as the inevitable end draws near. They also differ from religious narratives in significant ways, including their materialist conception of life and their social constructionist slant on meaning. Materialist conception refers to how the nonreligious reject supernatural notions of a soul or spirit that survives death in favor of a scientific opinion that consciousness resides in the brain.

While aspects of the deceased may live on (in the sense of genes passed on to children or an energy that reverts to the universe), nonbelievers do not think they continue existing once the brain is dead. Social constructionism rejects any inherent meaning in the universe. Instead, it is up to human beings to create purpose in their lives.

It is not only the secular who create their own meaning. The way people mix and match various sources is cause to pause and reconsider the lines between "religious" and "secular." Is an atheist who finds meaning in Buddhism becoming religious? How should those raised Catholic be categorized when they find Mass calming while denying belief in God or an afterlife?

Comforting an Atheist in Mourning

Too often, nonbelievers in mourning hear phrases such as "he's in a better place now" and "it's all part of God's plan." While it always is difficult finding the right words to express sympathy, well-meaning supporters may find it especially challenging to relate to bereaved atheists and think of what to say to help them feel better. Upon receiving religious sentiments, the nonbeliever not only is not likely comforted but also may feel further distanced from those offering such statements.

Here are a few thoughts that might be helpful when supporting an atheist. These suggestions apply for all mourners:

1. "I'm sorry for your loss." This statement is simple and straightforward but often overlooked. This sentiment can be powerful, as it acknowledges the person feels the mourner's pain and sympathizes with the experience.

2. "I'm thinking of you." In a condolence card there may be no more meaningful sentence.

3. Maintain open communication. Sincere questions are a good thing. A supportive friend might ask what he or she can do for the mourner. Everyone copes differently. Rather than explaining how the supporter feels or thinks the mourner should feel, the friend should provide the opportunity for the one in grief to share her or his feelings. Being able to express one's emotions is a vital way to deal with them. It is important for the friend not to fake it. If the friend is uncomfortable, he or she should say so. It is preferable for the mourner to know of the other's discomfort than to be avoided or offered empty cliches.

4. Simply be there. Having others around is comforting. Knowing that others care enough to be there is reassuring. Know that silence during grief is okay.

5. Share fond memories of the deceased. Generally, exchanging good memories is the thing to do. But if the deceased endured a lengthy, drawn-out death, those who dealt with it may need to share their experiences to process their anticipatory grief. Good friends will let them while offering their own positive memories. Funny anecdotes are appropriate. It is important to tell stories of how the deceased impacted a friend's life. These are uplifting recollections.

6. Even for atheists, the deceased can live on. On the surface this seems a contradiction. But what is meant is that the loved one can live on through the impact he has made on the world and on those who were part of his life. People needn't literally live on forever in order to live on through the actions they took while alive. Help atheists consider how their loved one will continue to impact the world even though they are no longer in it.

The carryover from comforting an atheist to supporting anyone of any faith is that the way people are treated while alive is so much more important than the idea that they will be seen again someday. That's a thought worthy of daily meditation.

CHAPTER 8

Many Modes of Grief

Mostly grief is thought of in postdeath terms. It is the pain and suffering experienced after a loved one dies. Several distinct, out-of-the-ordinary situations are worth examining.

Ambiguous Loss

Pauline Boss, professor emeritus at the University of Minnesota, coined the term "ambiguous loss" in the 1970s, referring to the experience of the loved ones of soldiers missing in action. The families of these combatants had no proof of their relatives' fate. When death cannot be verified or there is no certainty that the person will return to the way he or she used to be, the loss is said to be ambiguous. The mourner is in a psychological limbo, oscillating between hope and hopelessness. The mourner is stuck, unable to move forward with an expression of grief, lacking assuredness that there is anything to grieve.

Soldiers missing in action and unfound murder victims characterize such loss. Divorce may leave one uncertain of a return to normalcy, as might a loved one's diagnosis of dementia.

Disenfranchised Grief

When society denies one's capacity to grieve, sadness is compounded. Disenfranchised grief is unacknowledged in the mourner's world. Grief can be disenfranchised because of the specific type of death. When Kenneth Doka coined the term "disenfranchised grief," it applied to stigmatized losses such as suicide and to losses not generally recognized by society to warrant grieving. An executed inmate falls into this category (Doka, 187).

The term "disenfranchised grief" has expanded to include the sorrow of a sibling (Doka, 170). When a brother or sister dies, the parents of the deceased "own" the loss. A sibling's grief takes a back seat. The emotions of the surviving sibling can be marginalized. When others offer sympathy, they may quickly shift to asking about the parents. Sibling grief becomes secondary. Disenfranchised, siblings may be subject to this type of grief for years until they are able to process their loss.

However a sibling grieves, each experiences a sorrow outside the mainstream of primary bereavement, a grief shaped by the gender and birth order of the siblings involved. Sibling loss lacks research: each iteration bears its own signature of how the relationship developed.

Grief-stricken siblings might suffer loneliness as they endure unacknowledged sadness. Other emotions may be swirling. There may be long-harbored envy or anger toward the deceased sibling. Guilt too may be in the mix if the survivor was mean to the lost sibling or even wished the sibling dead at some point. Also to be considered is the effect that the bereaved parents' grief exerts on the surviving child. The grieving sibling may be resented simply for surviving. Or the bereaved sibling may be smothered by parents whose concerns cause them to be overly protective of remaining children. How parents respond may influence a child's development.

Should the surviving child have to assume caretaking duties for her parents, that child may feel the need to suppress her grief. A survivor's shifting relationship with grieving parents can bring about a confusing barrage of emotions and obligations that further obscure her grief.

Denied recognition, disenfranchised grief can haunt siblings for years. Lack of approval adds an awkward dimension to loss. Marginalized grief experienced by siblings when their loss is rebuffed may be displaced and surface in subsequent relationships (Doka, 173). When loss is frowned upon based on a family's or society's standards, the missing acknowledgment only compounds the mourner's anguish.

Whether twins or sisters and brothers born close in age or far apart, many siblings grow up together. They may develop a codependent relationship that can be mutually beneficial. Most grow up with similar family values and culture. When siblings become young adults, their concurrent lives together wind down. They likely leave the family of origin to live an adult life that suits personal and professional ambitions. Although the tightly knit years of growing up together are over, the collective history of siblings is embedded in their memories.

The genetic and experiential aspects that siblings share remain pivotal throughout their lives. When one dies, the loss obstructs access to the world shared as they were growing up, to memories of being kids together and being part of a family for all those early years and for all the shared experiences. Losing a sibling is losing part of yourself.

Grief That Is Misunderstood

Along with being disenfranchised, sibling grief may be forbidden. If a specific death is a subject not to be discussed, then the ensuing sorrow also is not to be expressed. Parents may go so far as to instruct children not to speak of their sibling's death. The difference can be stark between what parents, the primary bereaved, experience and what the secondary bereaved, the siblings, suffer. The biological connection and its significance in familial and social terms is what accounts for the difference in primary and secondary grief. The primary grievers' pain encompasses loss of all that could have been: the parents' future for and with their child, expectations of family historical continuity. Yet, sibling's secondary grief—marginalized, even forbidden sadness—also sparks anguish and should not be ignored.

Numerous variables come into play when considering sibling relationships, including birth order, age differences, gender, nature of interactions with parents and with each other, and cause of death. There are at least six different sibling pairings (not counting other siblings, if any): sister and sister, sister and brother, brother and brother, identical twin sisters, identical twin brothers, and brother and sister fraternal twins. Taken together, these variables present complicated challenges to comprehend. This aspect of bereavement deserves further examination. Sibling grief is significant. Losing a brother or sister can affect survivors emotionally, cognitively, physically, socially, and developmentally.

All factors influencing sibling interaction underscore the relationship's complexity. It can be friendly or adversarial. If there is more than one sibling, relationships are multidirectional. There may be a single parent or two or more when stepparents are involved. There may be same-sex parents. Family dynamics may center on a collusion with one parent against the other or a teaming up of siblings against their parents. However relationships with parents shape up, the lives siblings share operate in a universe of their own, apart from parents. Siblings may be allies or competitors. When a family is split by greed, envy, or dysfunction, sibling interactions can be painful, even marginalized.

Choice of profession, partner, or lifestyle can complicate sibling relationships. One sibling might opt for a career the parents view favorably, while another selects a profession the family frowns upon. Such differences can exacerbate sibling rivalries. Yet, even where family dynamics are destructive and animosity mingles with love, the loss of a sibling closes a significant chapter in the survivor's life.

Forbidden Grief

An extreme example of disenfranchisement follows the state-sanctioned execution of a relative. For such circumstances, the late Renny Cushing, a New Hampshire state legislator, founded Murder Victims' Families for Human Rights. His father was murdered in 1988, motivating Renny to work for victims' rights and criminal justice reform.

Renny had been a founding member of Murder Victims' Families for Reconciliation, a source of support for those who lost a loved one to violent crime. He sought to expand this group's mission by reaching out to the loved ones of condemned death row prisoners. He knew that "cause of death" on an executed inmate's death certificate read "Homicide." Renny realized the families of the condemned would experience grief similar to what the relatives of murder victims, mourning a loved one and in need of comfort, experience. The ostracism and isolation of those mourning one who has been executed is the epitome of disenfranchised grief.

The unwritten rules of disenfranchised grief determine who is entitled to grieve and receive acknowledgment, validation, and support in their sorrow. The stigma and pain of these societal expectations can be overwhelming when the mourner's relationship with the deceased is not recognized and the death's impact is minimized.

In addition to capital punishment, examples of disenfranchised grief include death of an ex-spouse, miscarriage or stillbirth, death of a nonblood relationship (coworker or neighbor), death of a partner from an extramarital affair, death of a gang member, and death of a pet. Situations in which death might be stigmatized include when the termination of life is caused by overdose (accidental or otherwise), HIV, or abortion or occurred during the commission of a crime.

Other losses, unrelated to death, can precipitate disenfranchised grief. For example, the impact of a loved one's diminished mental capacity due to dementia, brain injury, or schizophrenia may not be given due recognition by society. Similarly, infertility, addiction, and placing a child for adoption are all losses that may result in disenfranchised grief.

Anticipatory Grief

Grieving, of course, is about what one has lost. But another aspect deals with what one expects to lose. Anticipatory grieving is rooted in the future losses one expects to incur. Such grief encompasses many things.

One in failing health may have difficulty keeping her house in order and knows the time is near to be leaving her beloved home. Long before being uprooted, she may start lamenting the upcoming loss. Each distribution of a fond possession may trigger a new sense of loss.

Gifting treasured mementos cuts both ways. Giving away a knitting kit to someone who can make good use of it brings joy to the giver. But if the reason needles and yarn are being turned over is the giver's hands are too arthritic to manipulate the knitting, that is a source of sadness.

If one is facing surgery in which a body part may be removed or must deal with chemotherapy treatments that result in the loss of hair, anticipatory grief may flow from these circumstances.

A diagnosis of Alzheimer's can bring about preloss grieving for both the patient and loved ones. The inevitable changes accompanying memory loss affect all concerned. Living with Alzheimer's has been referred to as a "funeral without ending." As patient and caregiver cope with the present, dread for what's next can bring its own grieving.

In the same vein, a patient who is gradually parting ways with physical abilities because of age or illness may experience anticipatory grief, along with her caregiver. The slow but steady debilitating process has been called "the dwindles." Each noticeable loss is cause for its own sadness and can prompt grief for whatever may follow.

In the shadow of terminal illness lurks intense anticipatory grief. The inevitability is ever present. Patient or loving caregiver or both are apt to experience stretches when anxiety of impending loss is overwhelming. It is important to acknowledge during such difficult times that everyone deals with grief in their own way. The grieving of care partners—patient and loved one—may look very different. One may be reserved, while the other weeps openly. This doesn't mean they are not equally sad.

As Elisabeth Kübler-Ross discusses in her trailblazing research, people tend to die "in character." If, for instance, one lived life as an introvert, no one should expect a change of habit toward the end. One who has always kept his own counsel may not display the expected outward signs of grief. Others may feel that he is not facing his own demise realistically. The point is that both the terminally ill individual and those who love him are in grief, but the dying person is simply grieving in a way that is true to his character.

I witnessed my mother dying in character. Her last years were lived in a senior care facility. As she grew more fragile, she was moved from a small apartment to a hospital room. But at every station, even as dementia was taking over, her upbeat personality shined through. She expressed appreciation for any kindness given by the senior center's staff. I observed how her unfailingly polite, positive demeanor attracted the attention of the nurses. This is who she was, and no illness was going to rob her of her natural disposition. She died true to character.

Dealing with anticipatory grief is somewhat similar to how one copes with after-loss grief. But a few ideas might be worth considering in situations of anticipatory grieving.

A farewell celebration could be organized for a much-loved house before packing begins. Those who share fond memories of the place should be invited. Time could be spent retelling favorite stories of happenings in the house.

If surgery is in the patient's future, a shopping trip with a caregiver might be in order. The trip's mission is to scope out the requisite medical aid, such as a walker, before its use becomes inevitable. The idea is to get used to the device, start thinking of it as a trusted friend.

Patient and partner could go hat or wig shopping if a loss of hair is inevitable. Fashions could become part of a lighthearted conversation along with what their hair means to them and what this loss represents.

For those expecting the loss of memory, a "This Is Your Life" scrapbook could be put together with pictures and text. This could be a shared endeavor, with the patient and loved ones contributing.

Acute Grief

The initial response to bereavement, usually time-limited, is known as acute grief. This is a period of intense yearning, sorrow, and emotional pain. Distressing somatic symptoms may appear. These can include tiredness, confusion, and memory challenges. Difficulties eating and sleeping are common during acute grief. The experience dehydrates and literally drains us. Acute grief is characterized by physical, social, spiritual, cognitive, and emotional responses meant to slow mourners down and prevent them from being overwhelmed.

Generally, acute grief lasts three to six months beyond a loved one's death. Disbelief and difficulty comprehending the reality of the situation are common during this period. In her landmark book *On Death and Dying*, Elisabeth Kübler-Ross, refers to this stage as denial (Kübler-Ross, 51). The mourner's concentration is distracted by thoughts of the deceased. It is a struggle to focus attention. Forgetfulness can be a steady annoyance. The initial response to bereavement can include a loss of one's sense of self and a loss of a sense of purpose. Feeling aimless is common, as is feeling incompetent. Kübler-Ross also writes about the isolation from others and the disconnection to ongoing life that permeate this stage.

This book is meant to be most helpful to those experiencing acute grief.

Integrated Grief

Grief as a constant companion is known as integrated grief. This condition is a permanent and healthy form of grief in which the reality of loss is accepted. Bittersweet recollections of the deceased are readily accessible. The mourner's sense of self is restored, along with a sense of purpose and a strong semblance of well-being.

The potential for happiness is rekindled. Integrated grief brings a sense of belonging, of feeling connected to others. The new normal is a loss that is no longer devastating but instead contributes to a solid sense of ongoing life. This state of grief can make a mourner more empathetic.

My intention is that this book helps the reader achieve integrated grief.

Complicated Grief

In between acute grief, which may last six months or more and generally impedes daily life, and integrated grief, in which loss has been processed and while still present does not interfere with daily functioning, is complicated grief. Among the barriers to natural healing that can result in this sort of grieving are unhelpful thoughts and behaviors, difficulty with emotional regulation, and social isolation. A preoccupation with the more traumatic elements of the loss also can bring about complicated grief.

Complicated grief (CG) is a syndrome that affects up to one-fifth of those in mourning regardless of age. Proportionately more grievers will face the death of loved ones later in life. CG is marked by disabling, preoccupying symptoms that can last decades such as an inability to accept the death, intense yearning or avoidance, frequent reveries, deep sadness, sobbing, somatic distress, social withdrawal, and suicidal ideation. This syndrome is distinct from major depression and post-traumatic stress disorder, though it may coexist with each (Miller, 195).

Complicated grief may take hold at the six-month mark of mourning and is characterized by prolonged acute grief that causes significant disruption in everyday activities. Those most likely to be affected are the survivors of a spouse, a partner, or a child. Complicated grief can grip 10–20 percent of those in this category. A similar percentage suffers complicated grief if their loved one's death was violent or sudden.

Traumatic Grief

The risk factors for a traumatic death include a sudden, untimely loss that comes without warning. If the death involved violence, damage to the loved one's body, or the perception of suffering, it could be considered traumatic. If the death was caused by a perpetrator intent on doing harm, this could be traumatic for the survivor. If the survivor regards the loss as preventable as can be the case in the death of a child, suicide, or overdose, trauma may be integral to grieving. If the survivor considers the circumstances of death unjust or unfair, trauma may attach. In such situations, counselors should make space for complicated relationships. They should treat the trauma first, then the grief.

Traumatic grief may involve conditions of hypo- or hyperarousal. In the former, intrusive memories of death may accompany fears about safety. Anger and irritability often arise. Sleep issues, stomach pains, and headaches are common. Survivors may have difficulty shaking recurring questions such as "Did it really happen?" and "Did my loved one suffer?"

Hyperarousal manifests through withdrawal, numbing, and avoidance of any reminders of death. The survivor in this instance tends toward increased sleep and low energy while harboring guilt and longing.

Prolonged Grief Disorder

Prolonged Grief Disorder (PGD) is a condition distinct from depression and post-traumatic stress disorder (PTSD). The American Psychiatric Association included PGD in its revised *Diagnostic and Statistical Manual of Mental Disorders* in March 2022 (American Psychiatric Association, *DSM-5*). The diagnosis describes intense emotional pain that lasts more than a year after loss. Criteria include withdrawal, numbness, and inability to reengage with the normal flow of life. Those who mourn children are at greater risk, as are those whose loss resulted from violence, natural disasters, or other tragedies. Also at risk are individuals who have other significant life stressors or lack support systems.

PGD occurs in 10–20 percent of those who grieve. Contributing factors include a history of trauma or loss and a history of anxiety or mood disorders. Separation anxiety in childhood uniquely foreshadows PGD, while major depression disorders or PTSD may not be harbingers.

The identification of PGD is especially timely during a pandemic. Deaths from Covid-19 in the United States have surpassed one million. Covid's grim bereavement multiplier means that millions more may be at risk for prolonged grief. This sort of complicated mourning is to grief what long Covid is to that illness.

The official inclusion of the diagnosis follows years of debate over whether labeling something "prolonged grief disorder" pathologizes grief. Few survive childhood without losing something or someone dearly loved. The process of grieving a loved one is as idiosyncratic as the person who died. To indicate otherwise is to suggest that a normal process is a disease.

Lost in the discussion is what it's like to live with profound grief year after year. Society encourages survivors to suck it up and move on. After a brief bereavement leave, mourners are expected to return to work. When it comes to grief, there's scarcely a grace period. For that reason, long-term grief has been hidden from those who most need to acknowledge it.

The new diagnosis does not pathologize grief so much as make it visible to those who suffer it and to their supporters. Perhaps the best result from the new diagnosis is not the notion that long grief is maladaptive but that it is real for some, is a normal response to an abnormal situation, and is deserving of compassion.

It is often said of parents who have lost a child that they will never be the same. This is heartbreakingly so, as it is for anyone who has experienced a profound loss. But it doesn't have to mean that those mourners cannot eventually integrate that loss in such a manner that life again is meaningful and joyful.

To achieve that state of mind will require greater awareness on the part of the bereaved and those who interact with them. Recognizing when someone's behavior, even years later, might be grief-influenced could encourage more supportive conversation. Such awareness might lend permission to say "yes, it still hurts" when someone inquires. Survivors of some of the million-plus American Covid-19 victims are bound to benefit.

Distinguishing Between Grief and Major Depression

While the line between the two conditions is subtle, it is important to recognize differences. Grief may entail a loss of interest or pleasure directly linked to missing a loved one. Major depression is characterized by pervasive loss of interest or pleasure. One in grief will experience pangs of emotion triggered by reminders of the loss. A serious state of depression is marked by pervasive sadness across all situations.

A preoccupation with the deceased and a sense of guilt centered on death are typical of grief. A preoccupation with the loss of one's self-esteem and a general sense of shame can accompany major depression. It is common for one who grieves to avoid activities, individuals, and situations because of the death. Major depression can bring on an overwhelming malaise that results in a general withdrawal from people and activities. While intrusive images of the deceased are common in grief, they are not so prominent for those suffering major depression. What is more typical in depression are yearnings not normally felt.

Two of Grief's Unfortunate Companions: Anxiety and Guilt

Anxiety results from a mourner's attempts to control grief by repressing emotions. Anxiety increases as the realization sinks in that the situation cannot be controlled. During grief, one's sense of security, safety, and stability are seriously shaken.

Megan Devine, author of *It's OK That You're Not OK*, cautions that inside one's grief the world feels very unsafe, requiring steady vigilance (Devine, 146).

Under such stress, mourners should be given space to let out their emotions. Some measures to alleviate anxiety include lengthening one's exhale while focusing on breathing. The mourner might develop a mantra based on self-trust. Visualizing the best possible outcomes could help reduce anxiety, as could imagining a middle ground between what is a safe space and what is not.

Sometimes articulating exactly what one is afraid of allows mourners to frame their fears, creating a cartoon-like thought bubble into which they might stick a metaphorical pin. It also can be helpful to note what triggers one's anxieties. Picking up on past patterns is a form of anxiety mapping that can indicate early warning signs.

Guilt in grief can manifest as another expression of love, the sincerest wish that the worst didn't happen. A natural reaction—"If only I had ..."—comes with remorseful second thoughts. A mourner may experience survivor guilt: Why did my loved one have to die? Why not me?

Guilt can take other forms not mired in sadness. When one feels unburdened by no longer having to be a caregiver, relief guilt may accompany the realization. Joy guilt is likely to be felt at the first flashes of happiness. Such guilt can arise over the simplest things, such as a sunny day. Recognizing guilt and naming the relief can be beneficial.

CHAPTER 9

Grieving in Times of Quarantine

While I was working on this book, a global pandemic struck humanity full force. Covid-19's assault on the world disrupted my progress, as occurred with so many others. I was reluctant to research and write about dying when death was so ubiquitous. While I was overwhelmed with sadness for humankind, I felt that the situation was such an aberration that it would distort focus on "normal" grieving. The pandemic would pass, and life as we knew it would return.

But it occurred to me that this pandemic may be the harbinger of other plagues to come. So, while I was confident that science would put Covid-19 behind us, I decided that a chapter devoted to such unique mourning would be appropriate.

To be surrounded by so much death in a condensed time frame can produce dire mental health consequences. Adding to the public health crisis, a pandemic wave of grief poses its own mental health issues.

Rebecca Roesh, licensed clinical social worker specializing in grief, loss, and trauma, cautions that an overwhelming tide of ambiguous grief may follow a return to "normalcy." "Mourners isolated because of the pandemic have not had the chance to grieve collectively." Roesh notes that when society emerges from its coronavirus cocoon, ready to celebrate, mourners may be reluctant to burden others with their sadness. Their bottled-up emotions, whether loss occurred a week or a year ago, will result in complicated grief (phone conversation, June 1, 2021).

For the past century, Americans' response to grief has been to suppress the emotional pain and blunt its impact. Grief is treated as an individual endeavor, with the bereaved expected to "get over" their losses, primarily privately. The social isolation required by the pandemic has made grieving even more solitary.

Grief was not always treated this way. For centuries, communities came together to mourn the death of an individual as a loss to society. Victorian mourning rituals were extravagant communal affairs centered on customs that the bereaved and fellow citizens observed for months, sometimes years, following a death. Then came the twin devastations of World War I and the influenza pandemic of 1918. With so much death occurring at such a dizzying pace, mourning practices became prohibitively expensive, and social mourning was impractical to maintain. As with Covid-19, large public gatherings were not allowed. Quarantines were imposed. Funerals shrank in size, mourning periods contracted, and families grieved alone. A century later, grief again is widespread. Added to the deaths are

Field of birchwood crosses in a cemetery remaining from a small rural community abandoned 100 years ago, Meramec State Park, Missouri (2019).

other societal casualties: gatherings with loved ones, in-person education, and jobs that may not come back. Collectively, a way of life may have been lost.

Psychologists who study mass disasters such as genocides note a triggering in the brain when fatalities reach vast numbers. A "missing the forest for the trees" effect takes hold. Casualties expand into a mountain of corpses grown so large that it is hard to see the individual bodies. Experts claim that with the coronavirus, deaths have been hidden from the view of family and friends. This is a price paid for sequestering the ill in hospitals and nursing homes.

Compassion by the Numbers

In a span of weeks in 1994, hundreds of thousands of Rwandan Tutsis were slaughtered by soldiers and militias from the rival Hutu ethnic group. The response of the United States and much of the rest of the world was mostly a shrug. President Bill Clinton would later refer to his administration's inaction as one his greatest regrets.

Psychologist Paul Slovic was baffled by that apathy. As a result, he conducted experiments to gain insights into people's reaction to large-scale death and suffering (O'Hara). His researchers displayed a picture of a seven-year-old girl dying of starvation. The research subjects then were asked for donations to help the child. Another group was shown two starving children. Larger sets of impoverished children were shown to subsequent groups. Slovic found that people's distress did not increase with the number of children at risk; instead, sympathy often shrank. He concluded the more who die, sometimes the less people care. A sort of sympathy fatigue sets in. In greater numbers, death can become impersonal. Others can grow increasingly hopeless that their efforts can make a difference.

Hard, cold numbers lack emotion. Often emotion motivates action. With the coronavirus, the death toll in the United States surpassed one million by the summer of 2022. Yet, human nature may be working against an otherwise sympathetic population.

Public communication strategy suggests that to capture

national attention, an ongoing condition needs to be converted into a camera-ready event. Consider other disasters that have moved the public. When news crews revealed the devastation of Hurricane Katrina, people were moved to act. Compared to a single discrete event such as the destruction of New York's Twin Towers on September 11, 2001, the pandemic was a daily hazard whose sorrow has crept at a glacial pace. Oversaturated brains gradually tune out the danger.

The Look of Death

Absent observable manifestations, people may fail to be alarmed. Death unseen can be death that doesn't register with those not on the front lines. People can miss the connection they have with the death that is all around them, including their role in preventing sorrow's expansion.

Life lost during a pandemic, witnessed by precious few as precautionary measures prevail, has its own look. Patients may become ashen as their bodies battle for nutrients. Their skin grows splotchy, turning reddish purple as weakened hearts pump less blood to bodies that crave it. Often, the room that death is visiting is eerily empty as doctors and nurses strive to minimize infection. An oxygen compressor, pushing air to the patient's nostrils, provides a constant backdrop of white noise. The relative silence magnifies the patient's labored breaths.

A crushing loneliness hangs in the air. On occasion a family member is present, allowed to stay during a patient's final moments. Often patients are so elderly that adult children fall within high-risk categories.

E-Empathy

Every few hours for months, a Twitter account called FacesOf COVID shared snippets of profiles of pandemic victims. These passages personify the staggering statistics. Alongside text runs photographs of the deceased. The photos capture happy moments of people blowing out birthday candles, smiling with bowling trophies, and playing with their kids. The tweets are a way to publicly mourn the dead and display the death toll in human terms rather than cold numbers.

Since the launching of the Twitter account, hundreds of families have submitted photos and requested that relatives' profiles be posted. The responding tweets are a virtual receiving line for the bereaved, replacing forbidden family funerals. The extent to which families reply indicates how grateful they are to have their loss acknowledged.

As Covid deaths mounted, sociologists speculated the overall apathetic response can be pegged to who the victims are. The disease has disproportionately affected people of color. Those 65 and older account for approximately 80 percent of fatal cases. Prisons have been the sites of many of the largest outbreaks. Social scientists conclude that the demography of death has played a role in the lack of empathy. Empathy, they believe, is crucial in convincing people to take the necessary actions to blunt the virus's impact.

In disasters such as floods and earthquakes, those who escape often are the first to pull other survivors out of danger. Empathy flows instinctively. It may be the actions of fellow Americans that save one another. Empathy evolves from people putting themselves in the shoes of others.

Sociologists calculated that for every Covid-19 death, nine people are left mourning. Researchers based their estimates on age patterns in the pandemic's wake and US kinship networks. Close relatives were defined as grandparents, parents, siblings, spouses, and children (Verdery). Applying this "COVID-19 bereavement multiplier" indicates that nearly nine million people are in mourning with the death toll exceeding one million in the United States. These tragic numbers will increase until the disease is under control. Grief therapists anticipate a nationwide spike in cases of complicated grief, the sort that destabilizes an individual's life in significant ways.

Therapists speculate a corresponding increase in substance abuse and thoughts of suicide.

Making matters worse, there have been few formal acknowledgments of the lives lost and little recognition of the pain of survivors. After the September 11 terrorist attacks President George W. Bush appeared in New York City, offering condolences to first responders. The country flew flags at half-staff. The citizenry shared the mourners' sorrow. That tragedy took nearly 3,000 lives, about the number of deaths that occurred daily during the height of the pandemic. Unlike the sympathy experienced after 9/11, those grieving Covid-19 deaths have been caught in a partisan crossfire. Early pandemic skepticism disparaged the losses that some experienced. Half the country treated this loss of life as no big deal. The other half reduced mourners to a political talking point.

Perhaps the country is numb from emotional exhaustion. Perhaps the lack of empathy from the White House, epitomized by former president Trump shrugging that the death toll "is what it is" accounts for added anguish experienced by these mourners.

A Lonely Way to Go

What mourners experience during the death of a loved one is fundamental. A reworking of the survivor's identity is inevitable. Unlike a natural death, bereavement following a Covid casualty may be traumatically influenced by enforced absence. Not being able to offer a loving embrace during dying can distort a mourner's outlook.

Under normal conditions, humans are narrative- and meaning-seeking beings. A death resulting from Covid-19, however, tells its own story. The narrative is one of isolation in which family members are prevented from saying a natural, private goodbye. They cannot hold or be with one another at the time of death. They may not be able to separate themselves from the traumatic story of how their loved one died.

No Medicine Exists to Relieve This Grief

For a paper published in the journal *Death Studies*, psychologists Sherman Lee and Robert Neimeyer surveyed more than 800 American adults mourning the loss of a loved one due to Covid-19 (Lee and Neimeyer, 14). Their findings were startling. Two-thirds of respondents reported a grief they considered anguishing, preoccupying, and dysfunctional. They reported that their grief seriously impaired their ability to manage their children's needs, function in intimate relationships, or perform adequately at work. The raw pain of their grief and their struggle with underperforming in important social settings were linked to specific risk factors.

In follow-up research, the psychologists identified 10 factors associated with the circumstances of the death. These include distress about loved ones dying alone, feeling isolated by social distancing guidelines, and disappointment with the quality of the funeral or memorial service (Lee and Neimeyer, 14). These variables contributed to what the researchers called "pandemic grief," acknowledging the challenges of loving and losing someone in a health crisis. The psychologists believe that pandemic grief deserves its own name, distinguishing hardships that characterize this type of mourning.

Those surveyed reported experiencing a sorrow so profound that it has become their main preoccupation. The researchers believe that Covid-19 has violated the intrinsic need to connect, to embrace, to say goodbye. They note a forgoing of ritual that amounts to a disruption of one's world.

Potential Institutional Support

There is thought of establishing a White House office of bereavement care. Such an entity would break new ground by centralizing and coordinating domestic efforts across federal agencies. The focus of this office would not be limited to Covid-19 bereavement and would include those mourning loss from suicides, overdoses, and mass casualty events, among other unanticipated, traumatic circumstances.

This office would align with critics of officials who fail to go beyond offering posttragedy "thoughts and prayers." Many regard President Joe Biden as the nation's de facto commander in grief, as he has experienced the painful loss of his first wife and two of his children. Perhaps Biden can bring about change in how the country deals with mourning. An office of bereavement could ensure that Americans receive appropriate support and legal protections and that families are accessing federal benefits and could also coordinate action following mass tragedy.

Just as there is no concentrated bereavement support from the government, very few graduate programs in the medical or mental health fields make grief training a significant aspect of the curriculum. This void of professional instruction leaves grieving unaddressed.

A generation of children has come into consciousness during the Covid-19 pandemic. What will their takeaway be? The crisis encourages everyone to question their relationship assumptions. Who and what is important are values to be revisited.

A loved one's demise destroys survivors' sense of agency over their relationships. Death is out of everyone's control. But choices made in its aftermath can restore a mourner's power. Actively remembering keeps a loved one's legacy alive. Planting a memorial garden, listening to the deceased's favorite music, and cooking a favorite recipe are ways of tethering to the past. Proactive remembering facilitates healing.

Moving Forward Together

Underappreciated grief can put the nation in a precarious state. Grief can be cyclical, particularly near anniversary dates. Mourners may sense a drop in functioning at the one-year mark. This is common. As the pandemic persisted, death anniversaries and lockdowns were noted. One year isn't far along the road to recovery. It may be past the point when most nonmourners expect visible signs of bereavement to last. Collectively failing to exchange permission to express distress past a few weeks of loss can have troubling health ramifications.

In teens and younger children, reactions to unaddressed grief can include difficulty sleeping, anxiety, depression, behavior issues, and lower self-esteem. Grief ignored can lead to aggression and school struggles. In adults, unaddressed grief can surface as anger, anxiety, and depression. It may manifest as substance abuse. Suppressed emotions have been linked to other ailments including hypertension and autoimmune disorders.

Concerned individuals can advocate for professional help and acknowledge grief support as part of a basic social contract. This may ward off a looming public health crisis. Those who are grieving need understanding from friends and family. Their losses must be taken seriously, and their reactions to loss must be accepted without judgment. Empathic listening is key. This means listening compassionately from within the mourner's framework to stories of a loved one's life and death. It is important to confirm the pandemic's health threat if the loved one died due to the virus.

As in 1918, public health restrictions affect the practices customarily relied on for support and comfort. Funerals are stripped-down versions of what they might be. Some long-standing rituals must be abandoned. Some families postpone memorial services and their expressions of grief, preferring to wait until group gatherings are safe again.

Mourners should be assisted in holding on to whatever customs remain, even if that means holding a memorial service two years after a death. Rituals enable people to lean on comforts of the past while projecting a loved one's influence into the future.

New customs can be created. Everyday actions such as drinking coffee from a loved one's favorite cup or touching a framed photo when walking past can bring comfort when done with intention. Incorporating a loved one's values into new traditions can continue honoring the deceased's memory. Participating in public recognitions of those who have died provides meaning and context for the hundreds of thousands who otherwise might be minimized. Everyone eventually loses someone dear. Mourners' unexpressed sorrow can manifest physically and in interaction with others. Validating the bereaved at the time of loss is not only the compassionate thing to do, but also a vital investment in the common good.

In a time of isolation, it falls to the bereaved and their supporters to devise outlets for attention and to jump-start the collective healing process. Turning grief into action can address trauma. Covid mourners did this by prioritizing health precautions as preconditions and pushing for a more science-based response to the pandemic. Striving toward improved public health provides purpose for mourners. Saving others from a needless loss of life grants the satisfaction of knowing the loss of a loved one need not be in vain.

Developing a sense of community is another important measure in the mourning process. This is even more challenging when a pandemic subverts customary fellowship. Isolation exacerbates grief. In addition to obstructing formal rituals, imposed solitude disrupts a critical aspect of healing: gathering loved ones, connecting with community, and depending on others. Grieving alone is daunting. The touch of others is comforting.

People experience acute sadness following the death of a loved one. Eventually most mourners make peace with their grief, ultimately finding a way to keep the dull ache in the shadow of their lives. While elusive closure may never be attained, the normal functioning of life resumes. If, however, a debilitating grief persists beyond a year, it might be categorized as PGD, the most challenging form of complicated grief.

Under normal conditions, about 10 percent of mourners may spiral into PGD. In the aftermath of Covid-19, however, the number of pandemic-related diagnoses that started as complicated grief and extended into PGD likely doubled. Recall that the sociologists' Covid-19 bereavement multiplier is that every death may affect nine close relatives. So, the number of those experiencing complicated grief could be in the hundreds of thousands.

The Covid-19 pandemic has been full of factors ready to raise the risk of complicated grief. The resulting deaths have been unexpected and clouded by unanswered questions about the final hours of a loved one's life. Some mourners are shaken by guilt, wondering whether they carried the fatal disease into the household. Others resent the political opinions that the deaths are an acceptable trade-off for reopening the economy.

Another psychological roadblock is dwelling too long on alternative possibilities where the death didn't have to happen. "What if" scenarios are nerve-racking: what if more people wore masks; what if scientists knew more about the disease early on. In the midst of unnecessary death, it is difficult to find meaning. It is normal for those experiencing complicated grief to believe it unfair that their loved ones died, that they didn't have to die the way they did. When it is true, as in a pandemic, that's a major complicator.

The expression "ambiguous loss" was coined in the 1970s. The phrase initially referred to the experience of families of soldiers missing in action who lacked proof of their loved ones' fates. That notion is relevant for people who die in a pandemic as well.

A certificate of death establishes a degree of certainty while there is ambiguity about everything else. The bereaved are left to wonder what their loved ones' last words were and if they were in pain. Because mourners weren't there at the end, they may even question if the remains are those of their loved one. There are so many haunting issues.

The phenomenon of ambiguous loss impacts mourners in many ways. During a pandemic people grieve lost lives as well as other ancillary losses: security, serenity, social connections, and customary rites of passage. A pandemic produces a cascade of ambiguous losses. Some are difficult to pinpoint. People may not be able to put a finger on why they are feeling so anxious, sad, and confused. It is inherent in grieving.

Grieving is not something done well alone. A mass public health crisis may be the cause of grief, but its isolation only makes matters worse. Mourners are separated from loved ones on whom they normally rely. Traditional gatherings that provide solace give way to health precautions. While social distancing is an important safety measure, it eliminates the human touch that means so much when one mourns.

Taking positive action can be a way to combat the frustration brought on by isolation. Channeling energy by spreading messages of lifesaving public health measures can be therapeutic. Retelling stories of lost loved ones keeps their memory alive. Such devotion helps alleviate sadness. Conversely, dwelling on one's loss and stuck thinking about how bad the situation is interferes with the healing process. Accepting what cannot be changed while changing what one can is a prescription for recovery.

PART II

The ABCs
of Moving Forward

CHAPTER 10

Accept:
Entering the Valley

"Even though I walk through the darkest valley, I will fear no evil; for You are with me."—The 23rd Psalm

With each passing of a loved one, a journey through the dark valley of the shadow of death awaits us. We've walked this path before in our everyday losses. We're accustomed to the sorrows of those who make the trek: shock, disbelief, hopelessness, anger, and fear. The passage through grief will last as long as it must last. No shortcuts will get us through the valley. This valley may feel like a narrow canyon with suffocating walls. We grope through the darkness as we stumble across the canyon. Sometimes we sense that we are doubling back across painful terrain already traveled. We encounter the same difficult emotions with varying degrees of intensity.

In *A Grief Observed*, the British lay theologian C.S. Lewis, mourning the death of his wife, wrote, "Grief is like a long valley ... where any bend may reveal a ... new landscape." He notes that "sometimes ... you are presented with the same sort of country you thought you had left behind.... That is when you wonder whether the valley isn't a circular trench. But it isn't" (Lewis, 60).

From deep within the valley of the shadow of death, we might hear a coyote howling. We could find ourselves crying out for what we've lost. Intertwined with our grieving is another dimension of mourning and longing for our primal home. In some African cultures this yearning characterizes death as a homecoming. As we stagger through the lonely valley of mourning, our longing for divine presence is intense. It feels as if we are far away from home.

When the Saints Go Marching In

The primal urge to return home is central to the New Orleans tradition of the jazz funeral. Celebrating life at the moment of death with a drum-driven brass band is meant to reconnect mourners with their ancestral rhythms rooted in Haiti and West Africa.

In Ghana, the mood at funerals is nearly jubilant. An average funeral costs between $15,000 and $20,000. This price includes a casket that may be carved into the shape of anything from a beer bottle to a fishing boat. Ghanaians may spend more on a loved one's funeral than was spent on the person in life. It is more the merrier when it comes to attendees at a funeral. Some families hire fake mourners. Professional dancers may be invited as well to carry the casket and dance with it. The meal following the funeral is elaborate. Small appetizers are available throughout the day. After the burial, the family gathers to indulge in dishes such as fried fish with kenkey (a dumpling-like ball of fermented corn dough), jollof rice, grilled chicken, goat stew, waakye (rice and beans), okra soup, and tilapia. People with large families may cook the meal themselves; otherwise, caterers may be brought in.

The unusual New Orleans custom of the jazz send-off sprang from the burial societies of the Antebellum South. As a service to poor communities, funeral directors offered insurance policies to cover the costs of burial. In return for a low weekly premium, the insured received a casket, a service, and a burial plot. The fee included musical accompaniment. During the funeral service, musicians would wait in a nearby saloon until the bereaved filed out of church. The procession slowly headed toward the cemetery. As the mainline of mourners marched past, musicians fell in line behind them, thus, the derivation of the second line. The music moved the mourners' minds simultaneously in two directions. They celebrated their loved one's life, anticipating his journey to his next destination. The jazz also bound mourners to their past, their heartbeats in sync with the rhythm of their homelands (phone conversation with Michael H. Rubin, lawyer and Louisiana historian, March 17, 2020).

Letting Go

The way to rekindle what's left of our lives is to power through the valley of grief. The decision is in the hands of the mourners. They can cling to their loved one and bury their own future along with the deceased. Or they can loosen the deceased's grip and start the process of letting the loved one go.

Mourning is the difficult process of accepting the finality of physical loss in order to continue journeying in the land of the living. Eventually, mourners emerge on the other side of grief. Those forbidding canyon walls give way to a more gently rolling landscape. The valley floor expands into a light-filled welcoming space. The mourner is forever altered by this trek through the valley.

The lesson learned is that for something new to be born, something else needs to make way. After acknowledging what has been lost, after weeping tears of mourning for as long as necessary, one must let go of the gift lost to accept the gift of the next moment. The mourner's arms are not big enough to embrace both. One will slip the mourner's grip.

Sources of Sorrow

Nearly everyone experiences grief at some point. The cause of sadness may be the loss of a loved one, one's own good health, employment, a home, or a cherished lifelong dream. Whatever the specific source, mental health professionals talk about the significance of honoring rather than denying grief, of addressing rather than circumventing it.

At the summer camp run by Wendt Center for Loss and Healing in Washington, D.C., signs are posted to remind the young campers that "Grief Is About Remembering, Not Forgetting." How this is done is unique to each person, although the ground covered may be common to all. The anguish of grief will lessen with time, even while the aching sadness lingers.

Each individual holds grief in their own hands. Some clench

their fists, hoping this will keep grief away. Some find other distractions from their sadness. Yet, honoring grief encourages us to study its sources from the perspectives of both the losses encountered—deaths, diseases, and dreams—and what those endings mean: relationships, capabilities, and stages of life.

In her work *The Second Half of Life: Opening the Eight Gates of Wisdom*, Angeles Arrien outlines a way to work with grief. The anthropologist refers to this as "honorable closure" (Arrien, 135). Her concept is modeled on rituals practiced by indigenous people to commemorate endings and acknowledge their impact. Honorable closure is meant to draw wisdom from these experiences. To do so, a series of questions is asked:

> What am I thankful for from this experience?
> How did it positively impact me?
> In what ways was I challenged?
> Is there something left unsaid or undone that I must do or say
>   to feel complete?

The answers to these prompts inspire deep reflection. Out of grief, what have you created? This line of questioning opens an upbeat direction.

To become whole is rooted in awareness of all emotions, thoughts, and urges swirling within us. Consciously admitting one's feelings brings them into awareness. The first steps toward spiritual wholeness begin with such awareness. Simply expressing grief or anger is not enough. There are psychologists who encourage the verbalization of everything one feels, holding nothing back. This can perpetuate pain. There is a difference between expressing every emotion and fully feeling each longing.

Becoming cognizant of emotions without necessarily acting on them offers liberation. When one slows the process and studies the gap between impulse and action, one discovers a great freedom of choice. In an essay titled "Not All Tears Are Equal," Imam Jamal Rahman reflects on regaining balance. According to Sufi teachers, all feelings come from God and so are sacred. This is just as true of sorrow as of joy (Rahman, 40). Teachers of many spiritual traditions share this opinion, noting that feelings are simply energies needing to be recognized, tamed, and channeled. Humans grow more mature as they embrace both joys and sorrows. Avoiding sadness has risks. Spurned feelings surface and take their toll. It is essential to embrace the jagged emotions of existence.

There are lessons to be learned from pain if one is open to them. One must see suffering as a divine gift by accepting and incorporating its unhappiness. If one is willing to power through difficult spiritual processing, one will reap an unusual sense of freedom. Rumi, the thirteenth-century Sufi mystic and Sunni poet, jurist, theologian, and scholar, explained that tears shed on difficult days are the stuff of poetic metaphor. Where water flows life thrives, making tears sacred. In tender Sufi imagery, tears are water roses in invisible gardens and attract mercy. "Weep like the waterwheel," Rumi implores, "so that sweet herbs may grow in the courtyard of your soul" (Moore and Roberts, eds., 44).

A mythic figure from Sufi literature is Mullah Nasruddin. This popular character is a mix of simpleton and sage. His wise tales are treasured by Sufis for their lighthearted nature and deep insights. Nasruddin is timeless and universal. The earliest written accounts of him are from the thirteenth century, but his exploits were being passed along through oral stories as early as the eighth century. He is a Muslim of Middle Eastern origin, but because his wisdom knows no boundaries, he is considered a citizen of the world. Nasruddin's wit transcends time and space and is characterized by his popularity in contemporary China. Most of the Nasruddin tales are fictional but are based on images and metaphors of the Quran and the sayings of Prophet Muhammad.

Nasruddin is in sync with Rumi's assessment of tears. But Nasruddin adds that not all tears that fall are equal. He cautions that when the weeper becomes too attached to his tears, they lose their sacredness. While it is critical to acknowledge suffering and do the hard work of healing, it is also important not to be overly devoted to tears. At the proper moment, Rumi declares, one must let go of the pain and be sad no more. Sadness is blasphemy, Rumi cautions, "against the Hand of Splendor pouring your joy." He teaches that in extended grief, mourners must say to themselves at a certain point, "Enough is enough."

Just as it is sacred to embrace suffering, it is equally appropriate to appreciate blessings. One should be ready to catch oneself being happy. One should not neglect joyful moments and instead should acknowledge and celebrate them. Sufi teachers encourage their followers to honor happy moments and the blessings that come with them.

Breaking Down Grief

There are several important elements of grief. First, how do we know that grief is on its way? Grief strikes whenever we realize actual loss or detect an impending one. The jolt is most jarring when a diagnosis of a terminal illness is made, death actually occurs, and or we learn of a loved one's death.

When we hear a physician tell us that our loved one is suffering from an inoperable cancer, our hope for a cure is dashed. Our mindset braces for the doomed reality, and the emotions of grief cascade over us. Sometimes grief sets in at the moment of death. The realization is inescapable for the one who discovers the slumped body if the distressed individual does not respond to resuscitation or shows no signs of life. Grief flows from such encounters.

Grief is apt to be sparked as soon as one learns of a loved one's death, regardless of how much time has passed between death and discovery. A young man I know died while attending college on the West Coast. His friends got wind of the news and sent word East to his hometown. His college-age friends knew the sad story and shared it with their parents. But no one said a word to the family of the deceased. At first, no one wanted to believe that the young man actually had died. There was no confirmation. Maybe it was mistaken identity. Maybe somewhere along the communication chain somebody got the details wrong.

As the neighborhood hoped against hope, I called the university's dean of students. Anxious neighbors gathered. The dean would neither confirm nor deny speculation. Protocol must be followed, he said. The confusion created by the dean's silence heightened our anxiety. I insisted that he call us as soon as the authorities filed their report. In the meantime, the neighbors were torn. Shouldn't we go over and comfort the parents? But what if we got the rumor wrong and the young man is still alive? Or worse, what if the story is right? No one wanted to be the bearer of news that would forever change our friends' lives.

It didn't take long, though it seemed like an eternity, before the young man's mother called. Piecing together our interactions from earlier, she knew we knew. She told us what we'd heard hours before from the young man's friends. She and her husband were shattered, reduced to tears. Even though the tragic news had been delayed by several hours, that didn't soften the blow once reality struck. The pain of the experience, inevitably, makes one ask how long grief will last. Knowing that the hurt is temporary makes it more bearable. Setting a timetable on grief may be appealing but not practical.

Judaism sets markers that serve as gradations to the severity of mourning. The seven days from the day of burial are known as sitting shiva. These are the most intense times of grief; the wounds of loss are freshest. During these seven days the deceased's immediate family does not leave the house of mourning. Inclusive of the week of shiva, the 30 days following burial are called shloshim. Again, the Hebrew term corresponds with the number. Daily prayers are said for the deceased. The intensity of the rituals lightens. In my own experience grieving for my father, I remember not seeing colors again until the 30th day passed. I was struck by the blue of the sky. Until that moment, everything had been gray for the month.

The Jewish observance of mourning for a close relative extends for 11 months. Although not a hard and fast rule, this is often the time when a headstone is placed at the gravesite. This also marks a point when a mourner might engage in more lighthearted activities. While the time frame is useful, rabbis agree that no calendar can be superimposed on mending one's heart. Regardless of rituals, grief will last as long as it must. It preoccupies some longer than others. Determinants of duration include closeness of relationship to the deceased, how death occurred, coping skills, mourner's support system and resources, and what else is happening in that person's life.

Mourners may encounter well-meaning friends who hate to see the bereaved in pain. Such friends may encourage mourners to snap out of it, to push the process so that suffering ends. These friends likely have not lost a loved one. They do not understand mourning's therapeutic function or the downside in short-circuiting powerful emotions. When a mourner encounters such misguided encouragement, it is best to let such friends know that eventually grief will pass, but time is needed to process all the feelings. Those well-wishers can be reassured that when the necessary work has been done, the bereaved will rejoin them in the spirit of friendship. It takes time.

The prevailing theme of Megan Devine's *It's OK That You're Not OK* is captured in the book's subtitle, *Meeting Grief and Loss in a Culture That Doesn't Understand*. The text offers mourners permission to feel whatever they feel, to say and do whatever must be said and done when struggling with loss. This permission is liberating when well-wishers' insist that the bereaved return to being the person she or he will never be again. Devine's message is that grief should not be considered a problem to be solved. Rather, it is a mystery to be honored. There is a pain that grieving individuals may bear in addition to actual grief. That is the misery of being judged and misunderstood. This is especially painful when well-intentioned others are among the bereaved's inner circle.

While grieving should not be rushed, a competing consideration is that sympathy fatigue may be experienced by those who otherwise would be supportive. The pain of loss is authentic and unique to each mourner. Everyone sets their own recovery timetable. Even so, mourners cannot expect all supporters to stay sympathetic for as long as it takes to heal.

When my father died, I had just completed my first semester on the American University School of Communication faculty. My dean reached out to offer a shoulder to lean on. I appreciated his willingness to serve as a sounding board. His was a very busy travel schedule, so it was difficult to coordinate a mutually convenient time to meet. My mother encouraged me to get together with the dean sooner rather than later. She cautioned that though my pain would be considerable for some time to come, the longer I waited, the less urgent my need would seem to others. I found this an astute insight. The passage of time diminishes others' ability to identify with the deep grief of a mourner.

Grief's intensity can be inconsistent. While the feeling of despair may last from several months to years, it won't knock one off balance to the extent that it does in death's immediate aftermath. Grief's grip tightens and loosens, resulting in bad days and good. A mourner may catch herself chuckling at a joke, after which guilt descends. The mourner may burst into tears as a familiar tune reminds her of her loved one.

At some subtle time grief will subside, almost imperceptibly. This doesn't mean that there will ever be an end to the sorrow of loss. The memories and pain of death never go away. The passing of grief does not equate with forgetting a loved one. "Only time heals emotional wounds," so the adage goes. This is only partially true. Time is essential in the recovery process. However, time needs to be wisely used. Time spent avoiding grief will not heal.

Mourners run out of places to hide. Then, they must confront the void left by the death. Alternatively, if mourners invest time to mourn the loss, adjusting to a different life and identity, healing will happen more directly.

Circumstances Surrounding Loss

Everyone's grief is unique. The circumstances of each existence make it so. There is no uniform blueprint to apply to all grieving situations. There are factors, though, that can influence the duration of grief. Some measure of reassurance can be gained by knowing what these elements are.

The Significance of Attachment

To be in a relationship signifies a degree of attachment. What does it mean to be attached? The origin of "attachment" dates to the eleventh century and the French legal term *attachier*, meaning "to fasten." Earlier, the tenth-century *estachier* meant "to fix or support." Centuries later, attachment means much the same. The word describes relationships centering on security. This definition applies to children as well as adults (Archer, 48).

Adult attachment is influenced by one's early child-parent relationship. It begins when baby and world are new to each other. Writing in *Home Is Where We Start From*, Donald Winnicott observes that the presence of "a good enough mother (or parent)" is essential for a secure attachment to develop (Winnicott, 119).

The parent adapts to the baby's needs while allowing the baby to experience a modicum of frustration. To be securely attached is to be able to withstand separation. In a favorable setting, the child experiences real feelings and develops a true self. This contrasts with a false self that surfaces to please a parent and later others (Winnicott, 33, 65). To be attached securely is to develop trust in the world. This includes trust that the loved one will return.

How separation is managed by the parent and experienced by the child shapes how subsequent separations are handled. Separations are pivotal to many developmental milestones. Think first day of kindergarten. How separations are negotiated depends on the strength of the child's attachment to parents and caregivers. Ideally, the child develops tolerance for separation. As the child's confidence grows that the parent will return, increased stretches are tolerated without a feeling of abandonment. Attachments that strengthen fend off feelings of loss.

Survivors' attachment history shapes the form their grief will take. An early secure attachment will develop into a psychological strength that will weather challenges to the stability of self, even the ultimate separation of a loved one's death.

Mother and child statue, Bellefontaine Cemetery, St. Louis, Missouri (2020).

Mothers

However the relationship is depicted, mothers embody an essence that is difficult to describe. After a baby is born, it listens to, looks at, and smells the unique scent of its mother while nestled in her arms. No matter how the relationship evolves, a mother's presence is like oxygen. It may go unnoticed until it is required to breathe. Transitioning from always there to never there again, a mother's death is difficult to fathom.

At birth, the umbilical cord, the nutritional connector between mother and child, is cut. Similarly, at death the emotional cord between mother and child is forever severed. Even if the mother-child relationship began at adoption and even if the relationship grew shaky, she is there until she dies. Regardless of how her life ends—peacefully or tragically—a mother's death is the final cut.

Young Grief

While children's grief lacks understanding, it is still intense. A young child unable to comprehend death won't know why his mother isn't returning. He might even believe that his mother is close by, just away for a short while and will be back.

Grief can be experienced physically as a tummy ache, behaviorally as acting out in school, or emotionally as despair accompanied by crying jags. Fantasies may be clung to for a while but will inevitably fail. When they do, a child can be inconsolable.

Speechless

Early in life children are kinesthetic, using their bodies to discover the world. At this time the child has limited access to words, too young for language that later will embellish first impressions. Establishing secure attachment to the mother is critical during early growth. The failure of words in a bereaved adult can indicate a regression to the time before language, a time when everything was experienced through the body. For many, it also was a time when the child's mother was always there.

Word of a mother's death, no matter how delivered, is felt in the body. The brain transmits a message of distress that triggers a series of other brain reactions. Thinking shuts down. Executive functioning shifts to hold mode. The brain's automatic processing kicks in. Thinking yields to feeling. A mother's death can initiate a gnawing, relentless aching. One is left bereft when newly "motherless." Survivors are shaken to the core. Those left behind want to believe that she'll return. While struggling for emotional well-being, with unconscious connections activated to one's preverbal phase, longing is common. In the fantasy space between death and resumption of motherless life, one searches for comforting symbols.

To lose one's mother is to forfeit the self that once was with her. The lifeline that launched with the umbilical cord—or with adoption attachment—and progressed into a deep emotional bond is severed. Yet, a mother's essence, first internalized as the child's idealized version and later as the adult's more realistic image, can be a source of strength even while grieving. I got a feel for this when the rabbi explained my mother's interpretation of a burial ritual that troubled me. Even at the moment I was burying her, she was teaching me still.

The nature of the mother-child relationship can mend a broken heart even in her absence.

Fathers

How does a father's death affect his son or daughter? Some fathers die in battle. Others may perish in the line of duty, closer to home, as policemen or firefighters. Those who protect others outside their family may become heroes in the community or the nation. There are fathers who are heroes inside the family too. They are private heroes to their kids, who feel the loss deeply. There are daughters and sons who keep lionized, sorrowful memories following their dad's death.

The majesty and power of fatherhood has a place in art, literature, religion, and mythology. Well before Sigmund Freud conceived the Oedipus complex, the myth of Oedipus was the stuff of Greek legend. Sophocles wrote *Oedipus Rex* in the fifth century BCE. The play was about tragic King Oedipus, who sets out to vanquish a plague on his city of Thebes. Eventually he learns that unwittingly he has killed his father and married his mother, as the Oracle of Delphi had predicted.

More than 2,000 years later Freud, influenced by the intellectual sensibilities of Vienna and constrained by the inhibitions of Victorian mores, repositioned Oedipus's tragedy to suit his psychological theory. Freud's father died in 1896. A year later, he told colleague Wilhelm Fliess that "the oedipal relationship of the child to its parents was a 'general event in early childhood.'" Freud asserted that "it was an 'idea of general value' that might explain 'the gripping power of *Oedipus Rex*'" (Gay, 100).

In 1901 in *The Interpretation of Dreams*, Freud wrote about the meaning of his father's death. In *Becoming Freud: The Making of a Psychoanalyst*, Adam Phillips notes that when Freud writes that "the most important event, the most poignant loss, of a man's life" was his father's death, Freud was expressing how profound the influence was of his own father's passing (Phillips, 104). When his father died,

Freud wrote to Fliess that "by the time he died, his life had long been over, but in my inner self the whole past has been reawakened by this event. I now feel quite uprooted" (Phillips, 105).

From 1897 to 1899, Freud was intensely involved in self-analysis. His father's death and the Oedipus myth held great sway over his thinking, contributing to his sense of loss. The myth of Oedipus became as intertwined in the ethos of Freud's psychoanalytic values as love and work. This concept was central to his theories (Phillips, 26).

If the relationship is positive, a father's death is a tremendous loss for a daughter. She loses the presence of the first male figure in her life who encouraged and cherished her, who made her feel as if she could accomplish anything. A son, whose father was supportive and inspiring, can feel rudderless at the loss of his mentor.

Father Figures

Traditionally, fathers have represented strength, wisdom, and authority. Dads were around to fix things, know things, and bring home the bacon. Fathers embodied masculinity and understanding. Dads were up to the task and could be counted on to make matters right.

The picture of father as sole breadwinner and fixer seems out of step with current trends. It is more common for this generation to feature two-income parents. Fathers are sharing household chores and child-rearing responsibilities more with their mates, who may be the family's primary earner. With the fluidity of modern households, today's kids are growing up in all sorts of family arrangements.

In the changing environment of contemporary family configurations, fathers are scarcer. It's been noted that not only is the symbolic status of the father fading, but statistics bear out the impression of fathers' disappearance from the scene (Zola, xv). Given the data, research indicates nearly "half of all children grow up without a father" (Zola, 15). Children who are abandoned or experience other deprivations may spend considerable time conjuring an idealized image of their fathers. Such impressions may be fantasies built on who they would have liked their dad to be.

Even in situations where the father is present, some don't measure up. Some drink. Some rage and abuse. There are dads whose shortcomings get the best of them because their childhoods were difficult. Bereaved adult children mourn many kinds of fathers. Often grief for a lost father can be ambiguous and never ending.

Of course, there are many fathers who live with their families honorably, reliably, and lovingly. These are the dads whose image children cherish.

The Fatherless Child

What becomes of the daughter or son whose father dies? It is different for each gender just as it is for each individual. A daughter may retreat while grieving or fantasize about indestructible heroes. A son whose relationship was rocky might displace paternal conflicts onto others. This might take the form of quarrels or estrangement.

And what of the fathers who weren't present physically, emotionally, or spiritually? What grief accompanies the offspring of absent dads who die? Grief can be difficult to manage for the daughters and sons of an absent or abusive father. That man's death may be liberating, but such freedom comes with remorse and desire for what could have been.

No matter who mourns, psychological issues may emerge. Issues unresolved from early development may be reawakened. Later, age-appropriate issues may be reactivated. Grieving shares attention with the developmental matters that become part of the psychological work of sorrow. Grief can help the mourner grow. Grief also can cause one to fall apart. This sensation is universal. After the painful process of letting go of a father, the mourner is changed.

We never completely let go of our father, the symbolic figure of authority and power, the personal figure who loved and taught or who was missing in action. The living man is gone. The internalized one, the father who lives in memory, endures. Sons and daughters who grieve—perhaps angrily at first and then lovingly—enable their mourning to be transformative. Over time joy becomes possible, empowered by the knowledge of having loved a father now gone and of his having loved them.

Life Partners

Grief following the death of a significant other can be devastating. When someone loses a mate, all aspects of a shared life collapse. Physical and emotional intimacy disappear. The touch that sparks the emotional bond between partners is gone, to be missed forever. The special ways a couple's love grows over time are extinguished. The death of a spouse has been considered one of life's most stressful events (Holmes and Rahe, 76). Author Julian Barnes zeroes in on widowhood's despair when he asks, "What happiness is there in just the memory of happiness?" He reflects, "How might that work, given that happiness has only ever consisted of something shared? Solitary happiness—it sounds like a contradiction in terms" (Barnes, 86).

The anguish of emptiness penetrates every corner of the bereaved's self. There are survivors whose eyes tear up whenever their spouse is mentioned. Their mourning is fresh and silent. Their being strains to regain the lost embrace. They yearn for the familiar contact that can elicit the response once initiated by the lost loved one. There is a longing for the lost physical expression of affection. The attachment—physical and psychological—the couple shared dissolves into loneliness endured by the living partner.

In a relationship that grows to become a loving bond, the mutual understanding that develops extends beyond passions and intimacies. Psychological familiarity spawns deeper intimacy. A long-term relationship can achieve such closeness that one partner can finish the other's thoughts. Both may laugh at the notion that ideas can be magically conveyed from one to the other. This is akin to priming, whereby a song or movie title is recognized and elicits a similar response from both partners. Spending considerable time getting to know each other well can create the context in which both members of the couple have identical reactions to things.

Nature of the Marital Relationship

The grief experienced by a surviving spouse will be influenced by the depth of the couple's relationship. The number of years a couple was together, the quality of their everyday existence, and how they handled their emotions all factor into postburial grief. A key determinant is whether the emotions that most affected their interactions were tender or prickly. Was the couple generally polite but distant, not able to express feelings?

Each spouse is influential in the psychological well-being of the other as well as their own. Research indicates that in couples where the quality of life emphasized interdependence and personal growth, such quality of life survives a partner's death (Bourassa et al., 270).

Mates Left Behind

Widowhood never ceases. Yearning for one's beloved, thinking that the deceased may return, is an irrational, powerful impulse in death's aftermath. Ideas and words don't work well. The brain is overwhelmed with the situation's permanence. How does one deal with "forever" and "never"? "I've lost my mate" captures the heartbreak.

Identities are altered when one loses a spouse, from wife to widow, husband to widower. Unless one remarries, these terms brand a new sense of self. Those whose lives revolved around a spouse often are more acutely affected by their mate's death and may endure more distress (Archer, 239). For some, stress can be felt physically when grief is not fully processed.

When sorrow has been delayed or forbidden it may surface in the body, which doesn't forget what transpired. Some functions may be adversely affected. In extreme situations, the death of a spouse may be so crushing that it hastens the demise of the survivor. Fortunately, the life and love force of eros often sparks the survival instinct. This drive motivates many mourners in their recovery from the shock of death. When thoroughly processed, grief can run its course and eventually will calm. The will to live an altered life will prevail.

Heartbreak: Anticipated or Not

The death of a loved one becomes every survivor's hard-told tale, recalled in detail and related repeatedly in bereavement event conversations. Deaths that come unexpectedly warrant a different telling than those following terminal illness. An unexpected death might be due to a natural cause, such as a heart attack. It might be self-inflicted, as in suicide, which can catch even close friends and relatives off guard. An unanticipated death may be caused by an external event such as a homicide or car crash.

If a fatal prognosis is made, pain penetrates the heart of the survivor, the one who lives with a partner until death. When a diagnosis lays out an end-of-life time line, a vacuum is created in which death floats until it comes to pass. This vacuum may betray a glimmer of hope, a desire that the medical evidence is mistaken. A tension builds between the inevitable and the wish for more time.

The experience of such anticipatory sadness may be characterized as grief being the price of love, the cost the bereaved pay for their deep affections. What is grief like after the final goodbye? How much time must pass before grief loosens its stranglehold on the survivor? That schedule is unpredictable. The recovery period varies for each mourner. Past research suggested that 60 percent of the grief-stricken recover within a year. Newer findings indicate it can take two years or longer to recover from spousal bereavement (Brody, D5).

There is no precise time frame for a spouse's grief. Only the bereaved will know when sorrow is diminishing. There are indicators that change is coming. One sign of grief easing is the capacity of the mourner to accept condolences gratefully. Another marker is being able to think of the deceased without the wrenching pain it previously had (Worden, 77). Research results aid therapists' understanding of grief. But an individual is not a statistic. No grief-stricken mate can be reduced to a number on a graph. Studies provide collective data about averages and outliers. They do not tell the story of a particular partner. Life as it was known before a spouse's death, is done.

As sorrow sets in and then morphs, the survivor builds a new life, one without a blueprint.

Age of the Deceased

It is usually harder to mourn the death of a younger person than to grieve one who has lived longer. The younger the deceased, the more difficult it is to mourn. The natural rhythm of life is disrupted when members of one generation bury a member of the next and never more so than when parents bury a child.

When an elderly person passes, there is some comfort in recognizing that the deceased lived a long, productive life. That said, no matter how old the mourner and how long the deceased may have lived, when a parent dies there is no escaping the piercing pain.

A Child's Death

The death of a son or daughter defies the natural scheme of life. A child dying before his or her parents throws the life cycle out of

Infant headstone, 1921, Bellefontaine Cemetery, St. Louis, Missouri (2020).

whack. Parents nurture dreams for their children. Long-term thinking, conscious or otherwise, may include the younger generation taking care of the parents in old age. All expectations are overturned if a child dies first. When a child dies, a parent is apt to feel helpless, even guilty. The parent has been the lifelong caretaker. When the child was ill or aching, it was the parent who provided the remedy. To a child, the parent embodies strength and wisdom.

As exaggerated as these perceptions might be, the parent strives to live up to the ideals of this power figure. Yet, in the hour of greatest need when death arrived, the parent could not prevent the untimely ending. No matter the child's age or cause of death, a parent will feel the weight. Sometimes the burden is even heavier. If the parent was the driver during a fatal car crash, it is difficult to forgive oneself. If the child was abducted and murdered, anger directed at the perpetrator may be as intense as the parent's self-directed anger for not keeping closer watch. In such circumstances, guilt can be paralyzing.

The death of a child comes with special parental concerns. These issues differ from other mourning situations and include the following:

> Others may assume that the mother and father of a deceased child will be the best source of support for the other. This may not be so. The earth-shattering emotions inherent in a child's death can create intense tensions between the parents.
>
> Husbands and wives may not heal at the same pace or be on the same page in relating to the world. One spouse may struggle to function at work, then come home to a weeping mate. Upon reuniting the two may be out of sync, making interacting upsetting.
>
> There also may be an expectation between the two that one should know how the other feels. Although they know each other well, no one should assume that a spouse is a mind reader.
>
> When one spouse retreats without explanation, it may come across as rejection. Expecting a spouse to understand

inexplicable behavior is asking a lot. It is essential to verbalize feelings. Maybe all that's needed is a hug. If so, the mate should say so.

Never is patience more at a premium than with a couple coping with the loss of a child. Each spouse must remember that the significant other is in significant pain too. Any claim to selfish behavior that one partner can make is applicable to the other as well. Careful, compassionate communication is critical.

The mother's burden may be more intense. Added pressure stems from early childhood bonding. The nine months of pregnancy create a special closeness that continues during the first years of life. Losing this closeness is to be mourned. While nothing can bring the deceased back, the antidote for this tender grief is the mother's memories. Nothing can take these away.

If the deceased is an only child, a difficult dimension is added to the tragedy. A deafening quiet fills the house. Where laughter once was, now there is silence. A house becomes eerily empty. The realization sinks in that the parents are no longer parents. The death of an only child vies for the top spot in the order of stress.

Among parents' pragmatic concerns are what to do with the toys and clothes of their deceased child. To whom will they leave their estate? Even the dispersal of family photos and other mementos that would not mean much to others becomes problematic.

When a child dies, parents lose some of their future. When a child comes into the world, parents dream up life scenarios. What career path will the child choose? What sort of person will she marry? What kind of parent (to my grandkids!) will he be?

Parents know that the twists and turns of life necessitate changes in plans. But very few factor in the premature death of a child. When an untimely loss occurs, it is both the child's and the parents' futures that are dashed. A measure of immortality, achieved through the progression of generations, vanishes, another loss to be mourned.

Parents' sorrow may be heightened when milestones are conspicuously missed. Graduations, friends going off to college, classmates landing first jobs, and friends getting married and starting families are all painful reminders of what the parents have lost.

Invitations to the joyous occasions of others may be received. Those well-intentioned friends, wanting to share their experience, may not realize the heartaches that are being reawakened. Recipients of such invitations need to consider them carefully and sort through their emotions. Such invitations should not be seen as obligations or become sources of embarrassment. When it feels right, invitations can be accepted. If it is too painful, sending a gift or a card with a simple explanation should suffice. A little understanding by the celebrants goes a long way. The protocol on both ends of the invitation is delicate. The guiding sensitivity should be that it is preferable to be invited than not to be. It could be even more painful for would-be invitees to be omitted from such occasions because of their loss.

A child's death may be particularly painful if it happens during a turbulent family time. Sources of friction may be a child's acting out, may involve juvenile delinquency, may center on substance abuse, or may revolve around other issues. Whatever the cause, a life cut short amid unresolved tensions leaves unanswered questions and aggravates the sorrow of an already sad situation.

Thousands of babies die annually from the mysterious sudden infant death syndrome. These are deaths with no apparent cause. The death of an infant does not always evoke the empathy from friends and relatives that it should. The thinking of others may be that the baby wasn't part of the family for very long.

What others may not recognize is that the initial phase of life—

weeks, months, or years—is a period of intense bonding. The close attention given to an infant is both a heavy burden and a joyful privilege. The connection that develops will never be forgotten.

Losing a child is excruciatingly painful at any age. Grieving mothers may complain of arms that ache to hold their babies. Parents who have lost an infant may observe carefully toddlers of about the same age and wonder if this is what their child would be like had the baby survived.

There are a couple of cautions for parents mourning the loss of a son or daughter. Giving birth to a "replacement" child can have unintended consequences. The pain of the original loss may be so great that parents may be tempted to think their sorrow will be eased by substituting the deceased child with another baby. That plan is not likely to go well.

A human being cannot be replaced. The child who once was part of the parents' lives is special in her own right; she deserves her own place in the heart of the family. Through no fault of his own, the new baby could come to be disliked simply because he is not the person who was lost. What a burden it is for the newborn to try to live up to the idealized memory of a sibling he never knew.

Another consideration for grieving parents is to resist the natural temptation to overprotect surviving siblings. The fear that another child might die, while unfounded, is understandable. The living children will come to resent that they no longer are allowed to do things they once could. Parents who are too protective run the risk of becoming emotionally dependent and creating new psychological issues. Parents feeling tugged in that direction might explain the inclination toward overprotection and encourage the child to speak up when feeling smothered. Honest communication can keep anxiety at bay. With patience and practice, a parent will become more comfortable allowing children to circulate in their old familiar ways.

An aching chasm accompanies the death of a child. The world feels empty to the parents. What was familiar about the child and what may have been anticipated are gone. Silence where there was enthusiastic chatter is another aspect of sadness. There is no planning for the child who has no future. Grief overtakes the heart, brain, and body of the parents, who transition into a strange world, one without their child.

The death of a son or daughter is likely the most devastating loss one will ever endure. Parents live with a hole in their hearts that never completely heals. Such grief never fully subsides. Rather, it becomes part of one's life. Eventually, sorrow becomes more manageable and less overwhelming. But it takes time and a lot of conscientious refection.

Old Age

The death of a grandparent, though sad of course, probably won't trigger the same intensity of grief as when a relative of the immediate older or younger generation dies. The emotional impact may not match that of the death of the mourner's close friends. It may even make the mourner question his or her depth of devotion to this grandparent.

What this demonstrates is that grief varies by relationships and by causes of death. When a grandparent dies, one's emotional reaction may be influenced by the fact that this relative is a generation removed. Comfort may be taken from awareness that this is an elderly individual who lived a long and presumably fulfilling life. Unlike the passing of a young person, a grandparent's death is the natural completion of life's cycle.

Another factor lessening the intensity of this loss could be physical distance between the deceased and the younger mourner. Perhaps little direct contact was experienced if the two lived far apart. Given this situation, one should not expect to be overwhelmed by the death of the elderly individual. Sadness may derive from not having had the chance to know the deceased better. Other times the loss of a grandparent may be deeply felt. This is the case when the grandparent played a larger role in the mourner's life. Perhaps the grandparent lived close by or even in the home of the grandchild and helped raise that person.

The unconditional love between grandparent and grandchild can create the strongest of bonds. When death ends this relationship, the generational spread is minimized, and consequent pain may be immense.

While teaching on a college campus, the most common grief I observed was the loss of a grandparent. Regardless of distance, regardless of how long the elderly individual might have been suffering, there was likely a special relationship that ended and a loss with which to cope. Even if that connection wasn't close, the death of a grandparent is an indicator—conscious or otherwise—of other deaths to anticipate.

A grandparent's death makes a student aware of his parents' mortality. They too are getting older. Their deaths may be the next ones to be experienced. There is appreciation that with the death of a grandparent some family history is lost. Certain questions about ancestors might never be answered. These are reflections as a grandparent is buried.

Cause of Death

When loved ones have advanced notice that death is coming, they may engage in much of their grieving before the distressed individual dies. This can result in a slightly guilty sense of relief in when death occurs. In this case, postmortem grief may by shorter in duration.

The more sudden, unexpected, or violent the death, the longer grief may hold sway. When a relatively healthy person suffers a fatal heart attack, a car crash causes death, or a suicide takes place, the bereaved has no time to prepare and no chance to say goodbye. The out-of-the-blue nature of the event makes mourning more difficult.

Long-Term Illness

When a loved one dies after enduring a prolonged, painful struggle, the bereaved may well feel relieved that the loved one's suffering is over. A mourner's thoughts may turn more quickly to getting on with life. The intensity and duration of grief may be less than had death come swiftly, in which case lack of preparation time is compensated by the grieving experienced after death.

When caught in the throes of a loved one's terminal illness, it is common to experience conflicted emotions. One's heart aches for a cure while the brain assesses the reality of the deteriorating conditions. The hallmark of such situations is anticipatory grief. Maybe there is a moment for a mutually meaningful goodbye. Maybe not. It feels like the grieving process has already begun, even before death. The soon-to-be mourner has a sense of what life will be like without the participation of the dying individual. The bereaved may have had a chance to put final touches on interpersonal matters and draw the relationship to closure. The acknowledgment may come before death that this chapter of the mourner's life has concluded.

Sudden death, fraught with its own miseries, is free from the torment associated with long-term illness. Absent is the anguish of observing extended suffering or humiliation from physical or mental decline. Sudden death has none of the drawn-out emotional draining that mourners experience watching a loved one battle terminal illness. A close family environment could entail a disrupted home, with medical equipment strewn about, privacy sacrificed to steady visitors, and sleep swapped for the vigilance required to tend to the needs of a stricken loved one.

An odd silver lining of a long illness is that families get the opportunity to care for a loved one over an extended period. There is the precious chance to express love and say goodbye.

Sudden Death

When someone dies without warning, it can be devastating. A sudden, unexpected death leaves the bereaved bewildered. The news of such a death strikes like a thunderbolt, offering no time to prepare. Before reality has sunk in, funeral arrangements must be made. Although there has been no opportunity to say goodbye or get answers to questions surrounding the death, practicalities demand action. Which funeral home to engage? Who should officiate? Who will compose the obituary? Who will get word out to the extended family? And on and on.

In the dizzying whirl of unsettling events, the best a mourner may be able to do is set aside grief temporarily and focus on the mundane matters of the moment. Grief will hang in suspension, waiting patiently before overwhelming close family members and sinking them in sorrow. Sudden deaths occur in countless ways. The common denominator is that they happen unexpectedly. They can result from heart attack or stroke, car crash or drowning, accidental gunshot or intentional suicide, or any number of causes. War and natural disasters are sources of death that come with little notice. The more sudden and the more violent the death, the longer it may take to cope with the shock of untimely loss.

Those mourning a loved one's unexpected death might consider the following:

- Talk through what happened. Securing the full story from authorities or eyewitnesses may ease the mourner's mind. It will help convince the bereaved that their loved one is truly gone.
- Attend the funeral. If it does not violate religious or cultural mandates, the mourner might view the body. This too confirms death's reality. There may be serenity in seeing the deceased at peace that can contribute to closure.
- Reminisce about the beloved deceased, sharing memorable joys and sorrows. These are the meaningful experiences that bring people close. Mourners should be encouraged not to bottle up their feelings. This is the start of the healing process.

Suicide

There are numerous types of unexpected deaths. Some youths and adults not far removed from childhood die accidentally from drug overdose or other reckless decisions. These self-inflicted deaths can devastate parents with grief, guilt, anger, and unanswerable questions.

Parents who are confronted with their child's suicide may be taken aback by the anger they feel on top of guilt. These emotions are not unusual. They are part of what may be the most difficult form of bereavement (Worden, 185–88). By facing feelings of guilt and anger and confronting questions after a suicide and then expressing these emotions along with healing tears, parents can grieve.

According to Suicide Awareness Voices of Education, there are nearly 800,000 suicides in the world each year. It may be impossible to comprehend why a loved one would choose to end his or her life. Disbelief, as in any sudden death, may be strong and long-lasting. This impedes mourning. Such disbelief leads to pangs of guilt. This may have been a subtle driver of the suicide victim, as evidenced on occasion by suicide notes.

Then, there is the stigma that must be confronted when a loved one takes her or his own life. Social attitudes may have become more accepting of these events, but people still can be judgmental when it comes to suicide. Blame is cast either on the deceased for indulging in such a self-centered, destructive act or on survivors for whatever role they played in bringing about or failing to prevent the tragic ending. There are suicide survivor support groups that can assist the bereaved in gaining insight on the cause of death and on what might have prompted the fatal action.

A suicidal death is difficult to discuss. Survivors often complain about the reluctance of friends and family to talk about a loved one's suicide. It is common for those who find it distasteful to change the subject. Adding to aggravation is the occasional congregational official who refuses to officiate at services for suicide victims. Besides being cruel, this attitude heightens the guilt of survivors and prompts falsehoods about the actual cause of death.

A common misconception is that one who is so disturbed as to take his or her own life harbors the ill-conceived idea that certain individuals will feel guilty when the suicide occurs. More likely, those who take their own lives are so distraught that they have no notion of the pain they are about to cause.

Mourning a death by suicide may take a long, long time as the search for answers never ends. Trying to make sense of the death may be an impossible task, especially while fending off feelings that the bereaved somehow may be responsible for the fatal act. What mourners of suicide victims need to realize is that they did not cause the death. It takes much more than one person or a single event to compel another to end her or his life. A human being's existence is more complex. Just as one individual cannot get inside the head of another, one can never know the conditions that caused someone to self-destruct.

The response of a survivor may be similarly irrational. The sensation of guilt may be overwhelming. What could I have done differently—or not done—that would have prolonged the deceased's life? This is the sort of unanswerable question with which survivors may torment themselves.

There may have been occasions when one contemplating suicide, in a fit of depression or emotional instability, threatened suicide. The stress of such threats can wear away anyone's resolve. A response, silent or spoken, of "Go ahead already and get it over with" is not far-fetched. It is possible that when the death occurs the survivor might feel some relief. For a mourner who thought or expressed these sentiments, guilt is a natural consequence. Such expressions may be uttered by those who have observed the gradual grind that results in suicide.

Playing the blame game is another example of misguided emotion. Pointing a finger at a friend or family member whom the mourner believes could have done more to thwart the suicide generally proves pointless. Such thoughts could even be a way to distract from one's own guilt. Blame is a delicate matter. No one should assume responsibility for another's reaction to external circumstances. Suicide is never the only option to overcome adversity, nor does it stem from a single episode.

Another emotion with which survivors must contend is anger. Suicide is a violent act that damages many more people than the primary victim. Mourners are entitled to their anger. This rage must be expressed if the mourning process is to commence. Anger does not negate the survivor's love for the deceased.

The suicide of a loved one is difficult to process. The following suggestions can aid during this period:

- The bereaved should be as honest and straightforward as possible about the cause of death.
- Mourners should seek sympathetic supporters willing to listen.
- Through select interactions, it can be comforting to know that there are others experiencing similar grief.
- Mourners should make the funeral as meaningful as possible for themselves. Perhaps a letter might be written to the deceased outlining all the unanswered questions and frustrations. The letter could include an expression of love for the deceased.
- A mourner might seek a support group of like-minded individuals. Sharing experiences reenforces that the survivor is not alone.
- Above all, it is important for a mourner to be patient with themselves. It is good to acknowledge that it can take a long time to recover. The bereaved should leave room for hope. No matter the depth of depression, a mourner can work through grief and enjoy life again.

Murder

The website Our World in Data reports that more than 400,000 people annually are victims of homicide. This section of the book is of particular interest to me, as I've been working to dismantle the death penalty for a quarter century. I've written books and articles on the subject. I coproduced *In the Executioner's Shadow*, a documentary exploring multiple sides of the controversy. I've lobbied to repeal capital punishment.

The more I study the legal system's response to homicide, the more sensitive I become to those who've lost a loved one to violence. This extends to the families of murder victims as well as those who become mourners because their loved one has been executed. I try to remain nonjudgmental regardless of the bereaved's stance on lethal punishment.

That said, I have a strong suspicion that the grief suffered when a loved one is killed is likely the most overwhelming grief of all. The murder of a loved one requires time and enormous patience to process. Like other categories of bereavement, specialized support groups have developed to bring together those who mourn as a result of murder.

Nothing prepares one for the shock of discovering that a loved one is a murder victim. Seeing "homicide" listed as the cause of death, as it is on the death certificate of an executed inmate, is uniformly jarring. Many emotions are stirred upon receiving word of a loved one's murder. Disbelief that someone could take another's life is among the first sensations experienced. The bereaved wrestle with the horror of piecing together a loved one's last moments. Not the least of the emotions felt is rage. Intense anger will well up against the perpetrator of this heinous act. The offender not only has taken a human life but has also forever deprived the mourner of the companionship of someone who meant so much to the mourner.

Depending on the facts of the case, the mourner may fear for his or her life. Such intimidation can be paralyzing. The bereaved individual may feel helpless, uncertain where to turn for assistance. An understandable urge for revenge may overcome the mourner. If acted upon, this desire could result in devastating legal consequences. If left unchecked, this emotion could consume the victim's loved one.

While working on *In the Executioner's Shadow*, I had a graduate assistant who tragically lost her father to murder the year before our collaboration. Among the film's featured narratives is a story of amazing forgiveness. The parents of a young adult rape and murder victim fight to spare the life of their daughter's killer. My grad assistant told me how fortunate she felt that the couple was able to know who murdered their daughter. In my student's situation, the killer was still on the loose. This drove home one more emotional trigger for the uncertainty, anger, and helplessness of some murder cases.

When a loved one has been murdered, survivors will encounter a range of situations for which they likely are unprepared. How does one break such devastating news to young children, for instance? What will be the reaction should the mourner choose to view the body? How deeply, if at all, should the bereaved get involved with the legal process? This could include joining the search for the killer, attending trial if an arrest is made, or both. As in my grad assistant's case, a mourner may need to accept the possibility that the perpetrator might not be caught.

The nature of a murder victim's death presents a sharp attitudinal difference for the mourner. The mourner is not grieving someone who died naturally but rather someone whose life was cut short, a critical distinction. When someone dies, it is generally accepted as the natural conclusion to the life cycle. When someone is killed, there is nothing natural about it. The killer has engaged in a sort of theft, the literal taking of a life.

That rage would well up in the mourner is completely understandable. That individual has been robbed, through an act of violence, of a life precious to her or him. The lost life represents dreams, companionship, and joy. The mourner has been deprived of a cornerstone of her or his future. Such grief can be more isolating than other deaths. The friends of one mourning a murder victim may become overwhelmed. They may have no idea what to say or do to comfort the bereaved. In such confusion, friends may withdraw. They may even feel a tinge of guilt, thinking subconsciously, "Better this happened to your family than mine."

Reverberations of this shock can be immobilizing. Mourners and their friends may be unable to act. This makes the response of my grad student even more remarkable. As a college senior, she directed and produced a homemade documentary expressing her raw emotions. Not only did she film friends who had lost a loved one, but she also turned the camera on herself to capture her painful feelings.

Another caution for one mourning a murder victim is that the understandable anger could boil out of control. Misplaced rage could intimidate others, resulting in further withdrawal and isolation.

The circumstances surrounding a murder can compound grief. If a rape preceded the homicide or the victim was entangled in a drug transaction or some other felony, coping with the death can be more complicated.

Sometimes families set mourning aside, diverting themselves by channeling energy into the search for and trial of the perpetrator. No matter the depth of involvement in the forensics, eventually the mourner must return to the work of mourning and confront grief head-on. Putting emotions on the back burner while attending to legalities may have a detrimental effect. At some point the mourner must face grief. Deep feelings need to surface. But with the passage of time, others may assume that the mourner is beyond the immediate, painful stages of grieving. Friends and family may not realize that the mourner is just starting the process. Needing support more than ever, the mourner should let others know.

As in other mourning situations, talking can be therapeutic. Inform as many people as possible about the circumstances. This builds a base of support. For those coping with murder, these suggestion are also helpful:

- When visiting the morgue, the mourner should take others with her.
- If asked to identify the deceased, the mourner should get information on the condition of the body before viewing it. This may soften the blow. Viewing a photograph can be useful preparation.

  There are alternatives. If seeing the body is too difficult, an identification may be made by verbally verifying an outstanding feature, or a trustworthy proxy may take on this task.
- Planning a meaningful farewell, if the bereaved are up to it, is a way to create a final memory that overcomes the mental impression of murder. Bringing forth fond memorabilia and favorite music and poetry can help celebrate life despite tragedy.

  The idea is to prevent murder's ugliness from being the final memory. Planning this event may be more than the mourning family can handle. The service requires careful consideration.
- If the perpetrator has not been caught, the mourner may wish to assist the investigation. This may help solve the case.

But the bereaved should not take the lead in pursuing the culprit. Passing along information is the appropriate level of involvement.

Mourners need not be vigilantes and take over for law agents. Seeking revenge compounds tragedy. No good comes from additional violence. Assisting investigators, however, can be a productive way to redirect anger.

- If a suspect has been apprehended, the mourner may choose to attend the legal proceedings. Situations may arise in which the mourner has no choice but to attend. Either way, mourners may be motivated to confront the defendant and watch her or him be convicted.

It is also understandable if the bereaved want no part of the trial. Whatever the attitude, mourners must be braced for a painfully disappointing verdict. The National Organization for Victim Assistance can be supportive in coping with all eventualities.

I came across a certain bias when discussing my book *Grave Injustice*. For a time, this also was the working title of the documentary I coproduced.

When my colleague, Maggie Stogner, and I approached funding sources, their reaction was that the storyline was not balanced. Everyone assumed that *Grave Injustice* must have a left-leaning bent, that a defendant subject to a grave injustice must have received a punishment harsher than deserved.

When I explained that a verdict could be considered a grave injustice if a likely perpetrator received no sentence or lighter punishment than warranted, my point was well taken. Although they acknowledged that injustice could be perceived in either direction, if I had to explain it, the phrase didn't work as a movie title.

Note: After two years of spitballing titles, my partner and I came up with *In the Executioner's Shadow*. No matter where one comes down on the controversial issue, we all live in the shadow of the official charged with administering lethal punishment.

- One mourning a murder victim might submit a victim impact statement. Some jurisdictions allow victims to explain the ramifications of the felony on their family. These statements may be read aloud by judges prior to sentencing. Even when such statements are not read in open court, there is therapeutic value in writing one's feelings to work through grief.
- Mourners should know that there may be unexpected twists in legal maneuvers. Rules of criminal procedure may not permit disclosing certain information, as it could compromise the case. Evidence subsequently surfacing at trial may feel devastating.
- If circumstances allow loved ones to follow the accused from arrest to trial to conviction, what they experience after sentencing may be a return to deep despair. Legal proceedings may provide temporary distraction from the hard work of processing grief. Time becomes available to carefully contemplate all that has taken place.

  It is common for the bereaved to sense a loss of control as an avalanche of emotions cascades over them. These sensations are not to be resisted. They should indicate coping is again under way.
- Mourners should read as much as possible about homicide-induced grief. Insights gained from others can be comforting. It is reassuring to know that one is not alone in this sadness. Learning how others moved forward can help one proceed with her or his own life.
- It could be helpful to join a specialized support group for mourners of murder victims. Such groups are available in some communities. Where they do not exist, a local mental health center might offer something similar or initiate a program of targeted support. Local police departments also could locate the closest chapter of the National Organization for Victim Assistance.
- As with all grieving situations but perhaps even more so when the sadness results from homicide, it is important for

Gas chamber (retired), Missouri State Penitentiary, Jefferson City (2021).

mourners to be patient with themselves and the family and friends around them.

Grief is a highly personal matter. Everyone reacts differently. Some can't stop weeping. Others outwardly offer little emotion. Each mourner should remember that he or she isn't the only one coping with this pain. In a meaningful way, each bereaved person had a unique connection to the deceased. If grief overwhelms any of the mourners, professional support should be sought.

State of Relationship

A factor influencing the duration and intensity of grief is the sort of relationship the mourner had with the deceased. Was the connection a loving and fulfilling one? If the mourner is left with treasured memories, closure will be more readily experienced. If the relationship was rocky, full of unresolved tensions, grieving may take much more time.

Conflicted Relationships

Grieving will be far more complicated when the relationship with the deceased is characterized by conflict. Such friction can range from a single, upsetting dispute to ongoing and unsettling differences.

No relationship is immune from tensions. It can be particularly painful when death prevents the resolution of rifts. A dispute that is taken to the grave can be very troubling for a mourner. It can be helpful to share this sorrow with someone with the perspective of both parties. Unresolved differences may add to an aching heart. It can be comforting to know that many such conflicts eventually are settled amicably.

When a troubled child's life ends too soon, before he or she has been able to work through emotional or psychological issues, parents are deprived of seeing their loved one mature and thrive. Their memories of their child will be forever stuck in their offspring's disturbed state.

Another difficult grieving situation derives when the deceased may have abused—physically, sexually, psychologically, or otherwise—the mourner. Responding to a tormenter's death with resentment and anger is understandable. Complicating the pain may be that such violence is kept a family secret. Victims often suffer their shame silently.

It is common for one so resentful to feel isolated from other mourners, with no one to turn to as a way to unburden oneself. As glowing eulogies are recited, the deceased's victim may feel like blurting out her or his story. The decorum of the funeral likely will inhibit such an outburst.

The victim may be envious of other family members who apparently had positive relationships with the deceased. Amid so much praise, any doubts harbored by the mourner can evolve into self-blame. Such emotional chaos can result in a double mourning, once for the life lost and another for the loss of a relationship that "might have been."

Facing this predicament, it is important for a mourner not to keep these awful secrets locked up. One in such emotional turmoil should seek a sympathetic ear, whether a family member, a dear friend, clergy, or a therapist. Unburdening oneself should offer some relief. An ancillary benefit may be seeing the situation with fresh eyes. A silver lining could be the recovery of precious memories of good times together. A path may open to positive reconnection with the deceased. The more complicated the relationship, the more intense the grief. The more comprehension gained about complex relationships and confusing grief, the better the mourner will be at working through the process.

It is important to appreciate that the grief a victim experiences will be very different than that of others in the circle of family and friends. It may be an unbearable sorrow to which others cannot relate. In such situations, it may be nearly impossible to sit through the funeral service because of the scars that only the mourning victim bears.

It may be difficult to conduct oneself in proper mourning decorum when one is secretly relieved to be liberated from one's tormenter. In addition to learning as much as one can about grief and incorporating these insights into one's own process, this unfortunate individual should seek a therapist experienced in such situations. A local mental health center may also be useful in identifying an appropriate support group.

Unfinished Business

An awkward void will outlast unresolved issues between a mourner and his deceased loved one. A dispute left unsettled, abuse not resolved, questions unanswered or never posed, apologies not offered, and, worse yet, love not stated are all unfinished business that can haunt survivors. Such an open-ended agenda works against closure. The mourner is left craving completion of thoughts, conversations, and actions. Hung up on what is left to be done, a mourner's healing can get off track.

As others progress with their grief, they may not understand what is holding back the one fixated on unfinished matters.

The distance created by these different states of mind can generate another form of isolation. Mourners should be cognizant of their unfinished business. Once resolved, they can work toward closure. They may do this on their own, or if issues are too complex a therapist may be helpful. Matters may be simple and dealt with directly. These mourners carry heavy emotional baggage and require more time, patience, and support.

These suggestions are helpful for getting a handle on unfinished business:

- Awareness of what remains to be done is a good start. Perhaps a final "I love you" or goodbye needs to be said. Maybe the mourner would like to offer an apology for something said or done or not said or done. Jotting down a list of actions advances the process.
- That list should be reviewed, and each item should be carefully considered. What might the mourner do to tie together the loose ends of an incomplete issue? Different individuals have different ways of expressing themselves. Perhaps an original poem or drawing could conclude the unfinished matter.
- Writing a letter is something nearly everyone can do. The bereaved controls the content of the message. One can express dreams and disappointments that help wind down that aspect of a relationship.

  If the mourner can finish the letter in time, she might place it in the deceased's casket. This gesture can assist in longed-for closure.

  It may take beyond burial to write such a letter. Months or years may pass before the mourner comes to grips with the issues. Whenever the letter is composed, it may be buried at the gravesite or burned and scattered in the spirit of cremation. While the original note is buried or burned, a reference copy should be kept.

  This letter captures precise thoughts and feelings that the mourner may wish to share with a therapist or with others struggling with similar issues. Writing such a powerful piece may produce an outpouring of emotions and subsequent relief. It may be part of the final stage of grieving, or it may be the step that initiates a deeper process.

- If a mourner feels the need to have more ongoing exchange, he might converse with the deceased's photo. Close-up viewing can inspire whispers or screams or even apologies. Such interaction may provide much-needed relief.

Other Events Swirling in the Mourner's Life

The life of the bereaved, in the aftermath of a loved one's death, is not always conducive to commencing the grieving process. Sometimes circumstances conspire that overwhelm the mourner. Some external events are major. The death of another loved one occurring soon after the original loss can throw the mourner for an emotional loop.

Small-scale irritants can be blown out of proportion. A car in need of repair can weigh more heavily on a mourner than it otherwise would. A significant matter, like losing a job, can wallop a mourner to a far greater extent than it normally would. A bewildered mourner may not know what to address first or what trouble might befall her or him next. Sometimes, pressing matters determine what must be dealt with right away. Immediate concerns may delay mourning, although grief cannot be indefinitely postponed. The need to mourn does not go away. It will resurface at a subsequent time. Some complications extend mourning.

When a loved one dies, memories may be so painful the mourner feels engulfed by them. The death of a spouse or a child can be so devastating that a mourner feels unable to stay in the deceased's house. Too many memories are there, stirring too much sorrow. Thoughts of selling the house may accompany attempts to distance misery. A mourner who follows through may feel some short-term relief. Before long, the memories that the mourner is trying to escape may morph from sorrows to treasures. If the home has been sold, the bereaved may discover how much he or she misses the comfort of that setting.

A mourner should proceed cautiously when considering a major move. Relocating involves many time-consuming components: getting the house ready to show; working with an agent who may obliterate privacy by parading prospective buyers through the property; packing up possessions, which entails difficult decisions of what to keep; and then house hunting, securing a mortgage, closing the deal, and moving in.

Considering the mental state of most mourners—scattered, distracted, unfocused—it is not the best time to make such an important maneuver. There are changes often overlooked when the move covers some distance. The mourner unintentionally may be dismantling her or his support system. Left behind will be neighbors, friends, doctors, perhaps a congregation, schools, libraries, and parks, among other amenities.

Each significant item lost may cause more mourning. The bereaved should think carefully before thrusting themselves into the chaos of grief overload. They should adjust to the loss of a loved one before taking on new losses. With the passage of time, mourners may be better able to figure out what and where they want to be next.

The same advice applies to a mourner considering changing jobs. One would be wise to take time to adjust to life without her or his loved one. When one is in deep grief, it is difficult to concentrate on learning new assignments. If one happens to be in a no-choice situation and must find new work, that person may want to seek employment that is not overly challenging, at least not initially. A more challenging position can be pursued later.

Grief Delayed

The following situation is a corollary of unfinished business not between mourner and deceased but rather within the framework of a mourner's sorrow. The death of a loved one can leave survivors paralyzed by grief.

Individuals who become the rock of their family may find themselves in the unenviable position of tending to everyone else's emotional needs while also taking care of the practical matters of funeral arrangements. Providing the shoulder others lean on while making legal decisions and addressing burial details may mean putting off their own grief.

Keeping busy does not replace the work of grieving. Once the funeral expenses are paid, matters of the estate are resolved, and others have resumed normal schedules, the one who oversaw family comforting will have to confront her or his own grief. That's when the pain of loss will sink in. Such sadness may be accompanied by a sense of falling apart. No longer must this mourner put on a brave front. Now, courage must be channeled into self-healing. Passage of time by itself won't resolve the sorrow.

Ironically, assistance offered to others may compound the situation. Family members who are getting on with their lives may have no desire to revisit the painful emotions experienced in death's immediate aftermath. Mourners at the center of family mourning may find themselves isolated when they need the support of others, who are in a different mindset. The family's rock has been taking care of everything and everyone else.

Months or even years may pass, but submerged grief will resurface. This is fresh grief, as painful as if the death just occurred. These survivors need to be patient with themselves, express their grief, and mourn accordingly.

Systems of Support

The support surrounding a mourner will have a big bearing on how he or she copes with grief. Family members may respond to one's needs, or they may be in a different state of mind, isolating the mourner. Colleagues may be sympathetic or oblivious, expecting productivity as normal. Friends can be understanding or, if they have not experienced a loved one's death, may have no idea how to help. Those who are inexperienced with grief may be well intentioned but, seeing the bereaved so sad, may try to encourage the mourner to push the process.

The better the support a mourner has, the sooner he or she will recover from grief. That person still must take the time necessary to reflect, mourn, and adjust to all the changes that flow from such significant loss.

Personal Coping Skills

As one struggles with grief, it is useful to reflect how she has coped with past difficulties. Did the individual seek information and support, or did she ignore troubles, hoping they would disappear? Did she actively problem solve, or did she avoid issues, throwing herself into her work?

Taking inventory of one's strengths and weaknesses, understanding one's coping style, builds a base of self-knowledge from which one can function confidently. Honing the ability to deal with difficult situations facilitates grieving.

CHAPTER 11

Breathe

Navajos believe that all creatures are given life through *nilch'i* (holy wind). In her essay "Partingway Blessing for a Pet," Lynn Caruso observes that all living things are interconnected by the common breath of *nilch'i* (Caruso, 116). Caruso notes all living things sense the shifting wind. *Nilch'i* enters a being at conception. It is inhaled at all times. This holy wind exits the body at death.

During times of loss, it may seem that the world is still, that the breath of joy has ceased within mourners. As the Navajos break from burial grounds, their belief cautions followers to be cognizant of the wind. This force can be observed rippling the leaves, waving the grasses, and floating the clouds. The Navajos are reminded that with one common breath, all beings were created, and all will return with a single holy inhale. Members of the tribe are instructed to be mindful of the gentle winds and remain aware of their loved one's presence as the process of mourning unwinds.

Serenity in Stillness

Often the best thing to do in the turmoil of grief is simply breathe. At the most intense moments of pain, the best action may be to find a quiet space inside one's heart and be present with exactly what is. There is a wisdom to silence. Part of its power is providing room to breathe.

While it is natural to be afraid of emotions and memories that might surface, sitting with sadness is what starts to liberate the mourner. Before one reorients to life, it is wise to let the soul rest and allow the healing of stillness, of silence, to permeate one's heart.

Gaining Perspective

One way to get a better view of a situation is to take a step back and take time to breathe. This can result in removing one's ego from what is happening. In a silent, contemplative state, one may detach from, without denying, the events in one's life and their ever-swirling emotions. This detachment allows one to quietly observe each moment.

The process starts by witnessing the conversations in one's mind without judgment. The mourner should pay close attention to her or his breathing. Focusing on breathing brings calming perspective. Breathing sustains life and energy. One should be conscious of the flow of her or his breathing. In Hindu philosophy, which encompasses Indian medicine, martial arts, and yoga, prana comprises all cosmic energy and penetrates the universe at all levels. Breath brings prana into one's body and is conducive to all activities. Prana is referred to as the "life force" or "life energy."

Acquiring new perspective involves absorbing all the sensations of the moment, the sights, sounds, smells, and feels. This includes awareness of one's heart beating, the warmth on one's skin, the weight of one's body, and the movement of one's limbs.

A Buddhist Observation on Breathing

According to Buddha's teaching in the Anapanasati Sutra, being cognizant of breathing is a means of awakening to the nature of all things and arriving at spiritual liberation. In *Breathe, You Are Alive: The Sutra of the Full Awareness of Breathing,* Thich Nhat Hanh outlines 16 exercises of conscious breathing that were taught by Buddha.

Nhat Hanh was perhaps the second most renowned Buddhist monk after the Dalai Lama. A Zen master, poet, and peace activist, he was nominated for the Nobel Prize by Martin Luther King, Jr., in 1967, when both men sought to end the war in Vietnam. Nhat Hanh applied the principles of his faith to the problems of the world. He wrote many books, including the best-selling *The Miracle of Mindfulness.*

Nhat Hahn offers suggestions for the practice of breathing exercises. He explains the revitalization that comes with slowing down and getting in touch with our in-breath and out-breath. He describes the progressions—from awareness of the physical plane to mental and spiritual planes—in a way that easily can be implemented.

One such yoga-inspired exercise is a meditation practice in which breathing is the bridge to a serene state of mind. The technique is called anapanasati and was taught by Buddha. The Sanskrit term "anapanasati" means "mindfulness of breathing." Anapanasati is the process of feeling sensations in the body caused by breathing, practiced in mindfulness meditation. This meditation is one of the Buddhist methods most used, historically and contemporarily, for reflecting on bodily phenomena. Buddha taught this method of meditation to cultivate enlightenment, which in turn could lead to release from suffering. Dealing with suffering is a pertinent focus for one in mourning.

One centers attention on breathing, allowing the mind to move at will, without becoming occupied in specific thoughts. The practitioner witnesses thoughts without paying close attention to them. Thoughts move into the background like white noise. In meditation, one becomes an observer rather than a participant in her or his mind's conversation.

The practice of observing one's breath while disregarding thoughts is meant to distance oneself from the clutter of the mind. Engaging in this technique encourages the practitioner to discover an identity beyond his thoughts. He becomes present watching his breath. Doing this allows thoughts to come and go without developing attachment to them. This becomes a potent way to cultivate witness consciousness.

Thich Nhat Hanh recommends this exercise:

1. Set a timer for five minutes. Time may be extended if desired.

2. Sit comfortably on a chair or sofa, with feet firmly planted on the floor, body relaxed. Rest hands in lap and let elbows fall against the side of the body. Consciously relax shoulders, stomach, and any body part that feels tense.

3. Lengthen spine by pushing the crown of your head toward the ceiling. Spine should be straight but not rigid so that energy is kept flowing freely through the body. This guards against getting sleepy.

4. Once relaxed and centered, your eyes should be closed or opened slightly with an easy gaze downward. Bring awareness to breath, feeling it flow in and out. Breathing should be steady and natural.

5. Notice where your breath is felt most. Wherever that is in the body, that is where focus should be maintained. Be observant of all the sensations involved in breathing. Take note of things such as the temperature of the air flowing through the nostrils. Become absorbed in these sensations until breath is all-encompassing.

6. Should the mind wander, bring attention back to breathing with intention. It is natural for focus to slip away from breathing, as the mind can be restless. Taking note of this and gently returning awareness to breathing is part of witness consciousness.

7. If thoughts dominate the mind, try to let them go. Let thoughts float past like clouds. Let them drift as if blown by the breeze. Witness breaths while maintaining a straight spine and a relaxed body.

8. Simply stay with your breathing. Let the sensations of inhaling and exhaling calm and focus your mind. Observe the wavelike motion of breathing. This is where your attention should be.

When the timer goes off, open your eyes slowly. Return awareness to the room. Let go of the meditation and decompress (Nhat Hanh, 12).

Breathing Through Suffering

To the casual observer, Buddhism may seem like a pessimistic spirituality. Equating life and suffering could be considered depressing. But a key point is that without suffering, there can be no compassion. Suffering can lead to a release of fears and an awareness of great compassion. Such recognition is neither pessimistic nor depressing.

Becoming intimate with suffering does not mean moping around feeling down, upset with the world. Becoming intimate with suffering is letting loose one's sadness and joy. It is doing what must be done to help others. Compassion runs consistently through the world's religions.

In the Zen tradition, a practitioner awakens her or his body by breathing deeply. One's breath should reach down to the belly, to be felt in the stomach and chest with each inhalation. Body and mind are awakened. One becomes aware of how the body feels without being judgmental. The practitioner does not think of a sore back as bad or of free-flowing flexibility as good and just is aware. This awareness precedes thinking.

One maintains awareness of body for 10 deep breaths and then is ready to shift awareness internally. The practitioner might ask oneself how he or she feels. Is there sadness or joy dominating the practitioner's mood? The idea is just to be aware without attaching judgment. It takes time to cultivate this sort of awareness, as it is natural to become involved in one's emotions.

One takes another 10 deep breaths while keeping a keen awareness of her or his inner state. Then, an intention, verbalized or not, may be added to the practice. The Four Great Vows of Zen incorporate these intentions:

Sentient beings are numberless, I vow to save them all.
Delusions are endless; I vow to cut through them all.
The teachings are infinite; I vow to learn them all.
The Buddha Way is inconceivable; I vow to attain it.

These vows reenforce direction for all students of Zen. The traditional principles guide practitioners to attain enlightenment and assist all sentient beings who suffer. Muslims too set an intention before their prayers, though theirs is silent.

Those engaged in spiritual contemplation might consider establishing intention. It clarifies action and direction. Concepts that connect one with a higher purpose are beneficial. For years I've concluded my nighttime prayers with three requests:

> God, help me to be helpful to others.
> Help me to be the best me I can be.
> Teach me to treasure the gifts of a brand-new day.

CHAPTER 12

Continue Connection

"Death ends a life, not a relationship." So says Morrie Schwartz as he reflects on death and love in Mitch Albom's *Tuesdays with Morrie* (Albom, 174). Schwartz, Albom's college professor who became a lifelong friend and mentor, adds that even after the death of a loved one, the survivor still has memories and feelings, everything except the physical presence. The significance of this quote is the reminder that a person doesn't vanish after death. The deceased are remembered for their deeds and relationships, for what they meant to other people.

Schwartz illustrates the difference between humans and other living beings by holding out a dying hibiscus plant. The flower dies and leaves nothing behind, but a person leaves a rich heritage after death. The most meaningful aspect of this heritage is relationships with others. Morrie's quote is famous even among those who haven't read the book. It is referenced to help the relatives and friends of the deceased cope with their loss and move on, knowing that with the death of the body, their loved one isn't erased from existence.

Loved ones live on in the hearts of survivors. Affections don't change after death. The expression emphasizes the staying power of the departed. Fond memories should not be tarnished by grief. They are a precious present that the deceased has given to those left behind. The challenge for the mourner, which can be daunting, is how to love in relationship with someone who is no longer there. The adjustments that must be made are threefold: external, internal, and spiritual.

The external aspect requires one to think about his everyday functioning in the world, no matter how mundane. For instance, now all the grocery shopping falls to the survivor. Internal considerations revolve around one's sense of self. If a child dies, is the survivor still a parent? The third adjustment is spiritual. How does the death affect one's beliefs and values? These considerations raise the question: who am I now?

Continuing Connection Through Milestones

Family celebrations, particularly in the first year following a loved one's death, are challenging. Birthdays, anniversaries, and holidays are natural points of connection that can become painful reminders of loss. One who was central to the celebration is now missing. This absence spawns sadness and longing. Feelings of abandonment can fill the void.

Mourners should plan for these difficult days. They might spend such days with close friends and family. Mourners might ask those who care about them for their company and support. At holiday celebrations, mourners may decide that they are not up to planning the family gathering. It is appropriate to ask others to take on these tasks. Mourners must be honest with themselves and those around them. Mourners need not be strong for everyone. They need to be able to laugh and cry and take care of themselves as they remember their special loved one.

Material Connections

A common concern shortly after the death of a loved one is what to do with the deceased's clothing and possessions. Questions arise as to when and how to distribute or dispose of items. The task evokes discomfort. Some quickly empty closets and arrange charitable donations. Others cannot bear to touch possessions, dreading that grief will overtake them.

There are no rigid rules for handling clothes and other possessions belonging to someone so important to the mourner. Every individual, every family, can determine how and when to remove clothing and other mementos that represent the fullness of a loved one's life. The bereaved should avoid turning the deceased's room into a shrine. This can be unhealthy, especially if it goes on for a long time.

To overcome the discomfort, mourners might try removing belongings in stages. It may be helpful to sort through possessions and choose certain items to give to certain recipients: a favorite old sweater, a special book, or a watch. This gives others something of significance to hold on to as a way of remembering the deceased.

A mourner may want to attend to the handling of old possessions with another family member. In this way, the two might share memories and support each other in their sadness. Giving away a person's possessions does not mean that the deceased will not remain in the mourner's mind. Distributing the belongings of one who has died is a significant act affirming that life goes on.

The most difficult part is dealing with the memories. Recollections can be bittersweet, recalling happy moments along with sad sensations of missing someone special. These feelings are not to be feared or avoided. They are a vital part of the healing process.

The Magic of Memory

Memory is a creative companion, capable of distorting truth. Notions of selective memory and re-creating history derive from distortion. Memory also can capture essence and pass it to the next generation. People, places, and things that we lose in our lives shape us as much as what remains. Honoring memories is one way to pay tribute to lost loved ones. It has its place in the grieving process. It focuses attention on the intersection between mourner and lost loved one.

Sorrow, love, and anger may surface simultaneously. This recall should not be done to idolize or demonize the deceased. The departed should be remembered as they were, a down-to-earth blend of shadow and light. The Ritual of the Rose recognizes the fullness and contradictions of the life of the deceased. With long-stemmed rose in hand, thorns and all, the mourner stands beside a body of water. As fond memories are recalled, the mourner pulls a petal and tosses it in the stream. With each unpleasant recollection, a thorn is plucked and pitched into the water. As the rose grows free of all adornments, the mourner throws the remaining stem into the stream, symbolizing release of the departed loved one. This small, lovely ceremony of letting go affirms the reality that relationships are neither all good nor all bad.

Another way to reconnect with memories is to revisit places associated with one's broken heart. The journey to honor loss and maintain connection may result in an affirmation. This journey could be a walk through nature, perhaps through one's own garden. Gardens are vibrant spaces where the drama of life and death is played out quietly, daily.

The power of a natural setting explains why traditional Islamic gardens of Persia and Muslim India are final resting places for those who lovingly tended the vegetation. These gardeners were careful observers of the connection between heaven and Earth. Such deep involvement in the cultivation process may well have inspired two of the Islamic words for garden. One is *firdaus*, which means "paradise." The other is *rauda*, which translates as "mausoleum."

Will Grief Ever Let Go?

This is a fair question as one hopes to pursue renewal through grief. If grief is defined as an "intense emotional suffering," it follows that at some point grief will lose its grip on a mourner. Although overwhelming emotions subside, this does not mean that the bereaved cease feeling sorrow. It does not mean that the deceased will be forgotten. It does mean that the emotional knots tying up mourners eventually will be loosened. Time, patience, and effort integrate loss into a changed life.

When one is in the thick of grief, it is natural to ask when the light will appear at the end of this tunnel of sadness. There is no single across-the-board answer. Recovery will be different from one person to the next. The bereaved should dwell on their own individual objectives. What must happen for darkness to lift? Are these conditions achievable? Do expectations include never feeling sadness? Does the mourner expect a complete return to normalcy, to life as it was? Do some mourners think they will never again have the urge to cry? Any "yes" answer indicates unrealistic expectations.

Although exact measurements may not be applied to grief's duration, eventually most people recover. Some sadness lingers. But the sharpest pain becomes manageable as the mourner integrates grief into her or his life. The intense anguish of early grief fades, replaced by a duller ache that too will subside. Many people have staggered through devastating losses and regained their balance to lead productive lives.

Each mourner can craft a new life, different though it will be than before. Life's experiences, good and bad, change everyone. Life coaches often emphasize that there is more to learn through losing than winning. From loss can spring personal growth. If a mourner processes pain properly, he or she will become far more empathetic and sensitive to the needs of others. One's life priorities may change, shifting away from material matters to personal relationships and spiritual contemplation.

Face to face with grief, people are slowed by sadness. They budge grudgingly. They press forward because down deep they know there is value and meaning in living, as was modeled by those who came before. A faith percolates, perhaps from the subconscious, reminding us of life's transformative power. This force prods a mourner to stay connected to his deceased loved one. The future is forever altered. The relationship with the deceased moves inside the mourner's heart and mind.

Life persists with its remarkable transformations. As a butterfly emerges from its cocoon, so too may the deceased's spirit transform beyond comprehension. As nature's amazing changes occur, we might detect a steady life force creating continuity with unexpected twists. It cannot be overstated that grieving takes time. Necessary work and patience are required of mourners and those around them. Healing happens in fits and starts as mourners begin to piece their lives together. Because recovery happens gradually, it is easy to miss. It takes careful self-monitoring to see progress being made. It may take the observations of another to point out the incremental advances mourners are making as they move forward through their grief.

Getting Through Grief, Not Over It

Even though time is critical to healing, mourning is more than waiting for life to get better. Mourners can do things to assist themselves during trying times. Diet, rest, and exercise, the basics of balanced well-being in normal times, are applicable to life during mourning as well. A greater effort may be required to adhere to such guidelines given the distraught nature of the mourner's mind.

Diet

Food plays an integral part in the mourning process. The acute phase of grief disrupts regular eating habits and can last three months or more. Some overeat to fill their void. Others lose their appetite. Some may have a gastrointestinal upset, making food unappetizing. Grief may fill the mourner's throat, making swallowing feel impossible. During times of stress the nervous system shifts into high gear. Adrenaline and cortisol are activated, engaging fight-or-flight mode.

Nutrition is important. When a person is stressed, it can be tempting to snack on whatever's handy. It may be hard to focus on preparing healthy meals. Food may not be appealing during sadness. There may be no comfort found in comfort food. If it is too difficult to eat a well-balanced meal, the mourner may try to graze, spreading smaller portions throughout the day. Smaller, more frequent meals may aid in absorbing adequate nutrition.

Exercise

Brain benefits accrue from exercising, especially for the bereaved's memory and mood. Grief can tug mourners toward isolation and away from being active, eventually resulting in anxiety and depression.

There is much to be gained from exercise. Regular physical activity reduces stress and can keep frustration and anger in check. Exercise can be as simple as walking. It may require some equipment, such as a bicycle or treadmill. It may involve a social component, such as tennis.

Whatever the bereaved derives pleasure from should be incorporated into a steady schedule, with a good 30 minutes devoted to the activity at least three times a week. In addition to stress reduction, exercise increases one's sense of well-being and energy. It also can enhance one's appetite and sleep.

Rest

How does one sleep when he knows that as soon as he awakens, he has something dreadful to recall? How good can the quality of rest be when the sleep cycle only veils the awareness of painful loss?

Losing sleep often accompanies the loss of a loved one. It is common when a mourner lays his head on the pillow, that thoughts of his loved one bombard his consciousness. A preoccupied mind keeps one awake. An alternative scenario occurs when sleep comes quickly, only to be disrupted by nightmares preventing a return to rest. Grief alone can wear one out. A lack of sleep only exhausts the mourner further.

If restless nights are a problem, the bereaved needs to adopt sleeping habits to alleviate the tired state. The following provides some useful pointers:

- Go to bed and get up at uniform times. Following this schedule on weekends reenforces the rhythm. Altering an ineffective routine can break a bad pattern.

- Drinking warm milk can make one drowsy. This is relaxing and works as a natural sedative.
- If waking up at night is a recurring problem, one might give in to the wakefulness and leave the bed, perhaps read a bit, sip some warm milk, and then try going to sleep again.
- Light exercise before bed may or may not work. Some find it overly stimulating, preventing sleep. For others it helps them unwind, easing them into slumber. A light workout might be worth a try.
- Many find that a hot bath relaxes tensions and readies them for sleep.
- Listening to soothing music can distract one's mind from grief.
- Watching television in the prone position can lull one to sleep.
- Reading in bed may tire one out. Avoid stimulating stories.
- Napping can throw off one's sleep cycle. These daytime departures should not be indulged in unless necessary to catch up on sleep.
- A sense of familiarity is comforting. It may be difficult to fall asleep in a strange place, making it best to sleep in one's own bed.

   Issues arise when an empty bed becomes a painful reminder of the lost spouse. The mourner might try sleeping on the spouse's side of the bed. It may be easier to deal with one's own pillow being unoccupied. Another trick is to roll a pillow behind one's back, giving the impression of not being alone.
- Overcoming a fear of being alone in one's house at night could be an issue. The surviving spouse might experiment with leaving certain lights on or keeping a radio playing. Timers can be set so that devices turn off after one hopes to fall asleep. Locking a bedroom door and installing alarms may provide peace of mind.
- Asking the police department to inspect the house and offer safety suggestions could enhance a sense of security.

- Adjusting bedroom temperature may aid sleeping. Some find a warm, humid room relaxing. Others prefer a cool space to make them drowsy. Temperature is a variable that can bring better rest.
- Meditating can help relax one. There are books and training materials that explain the subject. Prayer can be a form of meditation.
- Caffeine should be avoided before bed. Coffee, cocoa, chocolate milk, and nonherbal teas have stimulants that can keep one awake. Also to be avoided are heavy meals too close to bedtime.
- Taking the time necessary to unwind before going to bed can enhance relaxation. This can be very helpful after a highly stressful day.
- Avoid forcing sleep. If one's spent a restless 30 minutes tossing and turning with no sense of sleep on the way, it might be helpful to get up for a little while and then restart the routine.
- Smoking cigarettes before bed can disrupt one's sleep cycle, as can drinking alcohol before bed. The products may help induce sleep, but once they wear off and leave one's system, the sleeper is likely to awaken.
- Computer screens should be avoided within 30 minutes of bedtime. The light emitted from electronics can be a source of stimulation.
- If falling asleep becomes a serious issue, the mourner may seek a physician's assistance. Prescription sleeping pills may be an answer. Sleep medications should be used cautiously, as they can lead to dependence. Pills can backfire and worsen insomnia.

Other measures to consider during difficult mourning are the following:

- Take a hard look at one's relatives and friends and determine which ones will be best to confide in. Nearly everyone is well intentioned. But not everyone handles another's grief well. Some personalities compound problems. The bereaved should steer clear of those who are not uplifting. People more naturally supportive should be the core of a support circle, those ready to guard against regression into grief.

- Seek and join support groups specifically tailored for one's situation. If the death resulted from murder or suicide or if the deceased is the mourner's child, parent, or sibling, support groups exist for nearly every category of grief. If the mourner is too weary to take on such a hunt, this is something a friend could research.

- Reading as much as possible about the grieving process is good for any mourner. From such information, one gains a clearer understanding of what he or she is going through. This should make the process less mysterious and less scary.

- The bereaved should find time to be alone. Friends may think this is awkward. But much of recovery is a solitary journey. Being alone to process what's being experienced is how one moves forward. Relief starts when one senses a reconstruction of life taking shape.

- Just as any hard work deserves a break, so should the mourner pause periodically. A visit with relatives or to a favorite getaway will bring a respite from sorrow. Returning to routine, one should not expect grief to have vanished. The hard work must be resumed. A little break may bring a different perspective and fresh energy.

- Mourners should remember to pamper themselves occasionally. The deceased may have been the bereaved's pamperer. The one who died may have performed special things for the mourner. Back rubs, flowers, chocolates, and so on will all be missed. The mourner must replace these little kindnesses. Doing so will bring a bit of uplift.

- Remembering to be patient and gentle with oneself is important. It cannot be overstated that grieving takes time. Delaying new duties and responsibilities during mourning is a good idea. Those who have lost a loved one already have plenty with which to cope.

- Grieving is not competitive. There is no need for one mourner to compare her or his progress with that of another mourner. Everyone is unique. Everyone's situation is different. Mourners should stay focused on their own process.
- Embracing one's emotions is critical to working through grief. Experiencing the pain as it cascades over one is an important part of the process. Mourners would do well to let their tears roll.

  Sometimes well-meaning friends and family will rush to comfort one who weeps. This may require the mourner to find a place to isolate so that he or she can cry freely. The more one can let out and express feelings, the sooner the recovery will gain traction. Knowing that professional help is available should emotions become overwhelming should be a comforting thought.
- Taking life one day at a time may seem cliché. But the advice never holds more value than during mourning's initial pain. Dividing time into manageable chunks, even down to hours, can make the sadness less overwhelming.
- While generally it is true that the first year of mourning is the hardest, the anniversary of a loved one's death is not a magic milestone. Things will ease a bit with the passage of time, but no one should assume that the one-year mark means all is well. Grief can grip a mourner for far longer. The anticipation of the first anniversary can be more difficult than the day itself, with its uneasy emotional buildup.

With that in mind, how do mourners know when they are turning a corner? Subtle indicators can easily be missed. Clues include when

- the mourner acknowledges death's finality;
- the mourner can reflect on memories both pleasant and otherwise;
- the mourner can appreciate solitude;
- the mourner can drive on one's own without crying the whole trip;

- the mourner can recognize that hurtful comments of others are made not intentionally but rather out of ignorance;
- holidays are something to look forward to;
- the mourner can lend support to someone else in a similar state of mind;
- the mourner can listen again to the music the deceased enjoyed;
- the mourner can attend a religious service without being in tears;
- time passes and the mourner realizes that he or she has not thought of the loved one;
- a good joke makes the mourner laugh;
- the mourner resumes normal sleeping, eating, and exercising;
- the mourner doesn't feel constantly exhausted;
- a regular schedule returns to daily living;
- the mourner can concentrate on what he or she is reading or viewing;
- the compulsion subsides to visit the cemetery regularly;
- the mourner can find something for which to be grateful;
- the bereaved can establish new healthy relationships;
- the mourner regains confidence;
- the mourner can conceptualize a future and begin to plan for it;
- the mourner can accept life as it is without reconstructing the past;
- the mourner can be patient with oneself in the midst of a grief attack;
- the mourner looks forward to getting out of bed to start the day;
- the mourner can slow down to appreciate the small things in life;
- the mourner can handle functions once done by the loved one;
- energy once invested in the deceased can now be rechanneled; and
- the mourner can acknowledge a new life and growth through her or his grief.

When one notices some of these behaviors, he or she can draw encouragement that life's puzzle pieces are starting to fit together again. This is an indicator that brighter days are on the way.

As mourners struggle through the grief, they sense personal development. With this growth comes greater empathy for the suffering of others. It is likely that others experiencing the pain of loss will gravitate toward the mourner who has been wrestling with similar sorrow. The empathetic mourner can become a comfort to others. The role of helper has its own benefits. Lending a shoulder to lean on affords the experienced mourner another opportunity to resolve her or his own grief. Offering support lets one know that he or she is not alone in dealing with sadness. Reassurance is found in accepting the universal experience of loss.

Why Is It So Important to Articulate Grief?

As with many unpleasant experiences, it is tempting to consider ignoring grief. Some think they can set aside their sadness and power through with their lives. Stifling raw emotions encourages them to surface later.

When these bottled emotions do burst forth, they may manifest in unexpected and self-destructive ways. Delayed reactions could be physical, such as ulcers, hernias, insomnia, back pains, and debilitating headaches. Other responses could be psychological, such as angry outbursts, depression, difficulties with relationships, severe anxiety, and even preoccupation with one's own death.

Among the most powerful feelings one will ever experience are those related to grief. Ignoring these sensations of sadness is an invitation to subsequent collapse. On the other hand, leaning into these feelings, identifying them and expressing them signals the start of recovery.

Thinking of Grief as a Process

The initial stages of grief are characterized by sharp, piercing pain that is emotional, psychological, and physical. Conceptualizing grief as a process gives one hope of gradually passing through the early phases of paralyzing sorrow. Grasping the process may serve the mourner well.

Elisabeth Kübler-Ross's landmark work *On Death and Dying* established stage theory in the American consciousness. The book was a major influence during the early days of hospice and palliative care. Kübler-Ross's thinking resulted in a shift in societal and medical attitudes toward dying. Stage theory for the terminally ill became the standard for forecasting and explaining the emotional variation of responses to one's own predicted demise. While the book was intended for the dying individual, it has benefits for the bereaved.

Many have commented that a critical issue with the stage approach is that the bereaved do not experience grief in five predictable phases (Worden, 39). There is no reason to think they should. The experience of being terminally ill and confronting one's own death is different from that of being bereaved and struggling to cope with life without the deceased. The author discusses five significant stages:

1. denial and isolation;
2. anger;
3. bargaining;
4. depression; and
5. acceptance.

When someone learns of a loved one's death, the immediate reaction generally is disbelief. The grieving individual does all he or she can to duck sad reality. When anger takes over, those who are grieving continue to resist reality and pose the question "Why is this happening to me?"

The bargaining stage is characterized by the survivor's irrational attempts to reverse reality. The bargaining partner, of course, is God. The negotiation follows a pattern in which the one in grief offers to do some kind, compassionate gesture in exchange for the Almighty's sparing the life of the loved one.

The onset of the depression phase indicates individuals' acknowledgment of the reality they are confronting. The final stage, acceptance, brings the process full circle. The bereaved no longer denies the painful reality, is no longer consumed by anger, ceases to negotiate terms of a bargain, and no longer is swallowed by depression. Instead, the bereaved begins to contemplate the death of the loved one.

A flaw in this blueprint, as Kübler-Ross admits, is its lack of precision. In sequence, intensity, and duration, there is no one-size-fits-all answer. It is wishful thinking to expect grief to follow a predictable pattern and then be done with the mourner. This anticipation can be aggravating for those longing for clear direction. The value of the analysis laid out in *On Death and Dying* comes from knowing that everyone's situation is unique.

Other authors offer different formulations for dealing with grief. J. William Worden delineates four "tasks of mourning" (Worden, 41):

1. accepting the reality of one's loss;
2. fully experiencing the pain of grief;
3. adjusting to a new environment in which the deceased is absent; and
4. rechanneling emotional energy into another healthy relationship.

The first task is acknowledging that the death is real, which must occur before one can work through grief. One must confront the reality that the deceased is never coming back. Because death generally is a fact that mourners want to deny, overcoming this resistance to reality can be a slow process. Survivors should ask themselves these questions: In what ways have you come to accept the reality of death? Are there ways in which you are denying this reality?

The second task is to articulate the feelings that flow from the death. While not everyone experiences the same intensity of anguish, it is important to note that the pain can be so profound that it can manifest physical, emotional, and spiritual symptoms. Mourners' reality checks could include asking themselves these questions: What am I doing to feel the pain of loss? Are there ways I am avoiding the pain?

The third task involves identifying and understanding the

various roles the deceased played in one's life, then adjusting to construct a new life. The areas of adjustment are external, internal, and spiritual. The external realm involves how the death affects the mourner's everyday functioning. Internal considerations are how the death affects the mourner's sense of self. The spiritual aspect centers on how the death affects one's beliefs, values, and assumptions about the world. Questions that the bereaved should ask themselves are the following: How have my life and roles changed since the death? What new roles have I had to take on?

The final task requires that survivors concentrate on their own personal development while forging an abiding connection with the deceased. While embarking on a new life, the mourner is not betraying the deceased. The relationship continues, though it is altered. Even as the lost loved one remains special in the heart and mind of the bereaved, mourners begin looking toward the future. They start to create a new normal. Questions that mourners might pose are the following: Are there ways I find myself investing energy in the future? How am I remembering my loved one while still moving ahead with my life?

Therese Rando in *Treatment of Complicated Mourning* breaks down her approach to mourning into six "R's."

1. Recognize the loss.
2. React to the separation.
3. Recollect and reexperience the deceased and the relationship.
4. Relinquish former attachment to the deceased and its assumptions.
5. Readjust to moving on in the new world without forgetting the old.
6. Reinvest.

The common thread of these approaches is the perception that grief does not stand still. It is a dynamic process that leads one toward relief of the sorrow endured in the aftermath of loss. Once mourners gain this awareness, they will begin to recover. The process may be excruciatingly slow, but the way will be forward.

CHAPTER 13

Decompress

The sensation of grieving is unlike any other ache. It starts from the heart and radiates outward. It is an incomparable emotional tension. A safety valve to release pressure must be tapped. While accepting, breathing, and connecting, decompressing also must occur.

Helping Yourself

A primary piece of advice for mourners is to be kind to and patient with themselves. Burdening oneself with high expectations hinders the process. When grieving, mourners should not overload their workday. They should take on assignments in small, manageable units.

Mourners should let relatives, friends and coworkers know what has transpired. The survivor's denial or the circumstances surrounding a death may make it awkward to share details. Discussing a suicide or a homicide can be difficult due to the stigma that may be attached. The bereaved should try to explain to others how they might be helpful. Covering daily chores such as making a meal or walking the dog can provide relief. Being a good listener is an excellent way to be supportive.

Mourners may ask others to serve as their mirror. In their eyes, how does the mourner look? Does the mourner's behavior raise concerns? The mourner should take in the perspectives of friends and family and give those views careful consideration. Maybe they have a point. Maybe they're off base. Either way, these opinions are worth taking into account.

Talk therapy need not be reserved only for professionals. Mourners can share experiences with anyone with whom they are comfortable. At times a mourner may open up more easily to a stranger than to a relative. Talking provides an energy release and an emotional outlet. Bottling up feelings can lead to the sensation that one might explode. Expressing one's thoughts also can help clarify and validate a situation.

Relaxing, if only briefly, can prove beneficial. Simple exercises that focus on breathing and stretching help reduce stress. Relaxation can be achieved through a favorite activity. Hobbies may be active, such as biking and cooking, or they may be passive, such as reading and listening to music. Whatever the preferred pastime, it can provide needed release.

Eating a healthy diet is a must when one is grieving. Steering clear of junk food and consuming nutritious meals provides energy for healing. Such conscientious eating also can enhance one's mood.

Exercising is another important aspect of recovery. One needn't be too ambitious. But a daily regimen calling for 30 minutes of cardiovascular activity can strengthen one's well-being and brighten one's outlook. Finding a sport or exercise routine one enjoys is key to success. If the activity is dreaded, it will not be maintained. Exercise can be undertaken alone or with others. Mourners should determine which setting works best for them. Joining a health club may provide helpful motivation.

Mourners should maintain activities in which they were engaged before the present situation. If those endeavors used to be meaningful, likely they still are. Perhaps involvement level needs to be scaled back to avoid being overwhelmed. But mourners should not forsake such activities. Group or club memberships should be continued if the mourner finds value in them. Such organizations can provide structure to the mourner's life and be a source of personal contacts and support.

Walking for Healing and Other Emotional Outlets

Walking is an activity that can bridge the physical and the spiritual. If done with purpose, walking can be meditative. Walking a labyrinth can cover a lot of ground in a small space. The labyrinth walk is imbued with meaning and metaphor. The labyrinth itself can symbolize a journey, a conscious seeking of the life force.

Taking the initial step into the labyrinth is to allow oneself to be vulnerable by risking discovery of what's at the very core of one's being. The beauty of the labyrinth is that there are no wrong turns. The walker/seeker cannot lose her or his way. By staying on path and following the various turns, one eventually finds one's symbolic center.

When someone dies, it is natural to wonder how a higher power could let this happen. It is easy to overlook that death is a part of life. One becomes angry with the higher being or life force, however defined. Anger is particularly powerful when the deceased is a child, a parent, or a partner. Such anger is okay. It may even be therapeutic to rant and rave. Being angry is a necessary phase of grieving, something not to be denied.

Weeping is a natural expression of profound sadness. Even so, many grow up in a culture that frowns on crying. It may be seen as weakness. When we lose a loved one, it is only right to grieve. In some cultures, there are women who have the specific responsibility of grieving. They cry and wail and make moaning sounds. These women lead others in the mourning process. When mourners walk the labyrinth following the death of a loved one, they can use the meditation time to grieve by moaning audibly. With the whole body, mourners can wail and cry.

One should honor the body's need to fully experience the depth of sorrow from the loss of a loved one. The closer the relationship, the longer the grieving may take. One might visit the labyrinth monthly for a year with the sole intention of walking through grief. To maximize the labyrinth experience, one might place mementos of the deceased in the center of the path. The items may be adorned with candles and flowers. On the walk in, one might recite a favorite prayer or psalm or repeat a special word or phrase as a mantra.

Mourners should allow time to recall their own life and the departed's and reflect on how these existences blessed each other. A flow of tears may well accompany these moments. At the labyrinth's center, the special mementos may be embraced, embellishing the experience. The outward walk may be done silently, or a favorite song might be sung.

The Valley of the Shadow

Entering and exiting the labyrinth is good practice for walking through the "valley of the shadow of death." This valley can be a devastating place. But its intense darkness need not be permanent. Although what has been lost is never to be recovered, the valley also is a place of healing.

Time spent in sorrow cannot be rushed. Healing requires patience, more than mourners may think they have. But glossing over grief will not heal. Mourners should give themselves permission to be sad, despite all the pressures to be "all right" before it is time. Mourners also should hang onto hope that healing will happen even when the valley is darkest.

Cautionary Signs

When death occurs, other issues swirling about a mourner's life may complicate grief. Time, energy, and attention may be squeezed by other issues. Circumstances can conspire to overwhelm a mourner. The details of a loved one's death may compound the shock of loss.

Sometimes intense grief drags on for months. Watch for the following symptoms:

- haunting recurring memories that interrupt work, daily life, and sleep;
- flashbacks and hallucinations;
- gripping anxiety when a similar event is brought to one's attention;
- resisting thoughts and feelings related to the death;

- preoccupation with the death many months after it happened;
- overidealization of the deceased and overly romanticized recollections of the relationship extending for too long and too intensely;
- blank spots in one's memory leading to faulty recall;
- noticeable, lengthy loss of interest in events at work or at home;
- depression compounded by loneliness, hopelessness, and sorrow;
- separation from others leading to isolation;
- recurring survivor's guilt, evidenced by subconscious, gnawing questions such as "Why my loved one?" and "Why wasn't it me who died?";
- self-defeating, even self-destructive behavior;
- flat emotions characterized by an inability to experience joy or love;
- avoiding intimate relationships for fear of being left alone again;
- being overcome by emotions to the point of feeling a loss of control;
- hopelessness for the future, a sense that things will never work out in one's career or relationships;
- alcohol or drug abuse creeping into one's life;
- difficulty falling or staying asleep or sleeping too much;
- excessive irritability with others, leading to angry outbursts;
- difficulty concentrating on activities previously enjoyed;
- difficulty focusing on work, leading to performance disruptions;
- inability to relax;
- constant anticipation of what may go wrong next;
- being constantly on edge, overreacting to the slightest startling sound; and
- breaking into cold sweats or experiencing shortness of breath or a revved heartbeat when reminded of the death.

Many of these manifestations are normal, not requiring special attention. Symptoms may vanish in days or weeks. If they linger or become overwhelming, however, those behaviors may need to be watched closely. If the bereaved believes that any of these issues is lasting too long, seeking professional help is in order. This is especially true if the mourner is harboring thoughts of harming oneself.

Expert counseling is also merited if the survivor is dealing with a combination of symptoms, persistent for a month, while the death occurred six months or more before. This situation could call for an evaluation from a professional therapist.

The trauma experienced after a difficult death may be so devastating that it resembles PTSD. Akin to the psychological scars soldiers suffer after battles, PTSD can evolve when a person endures a painful experience beyond the scope of her or his coping skills. This syndrome is an appropriate self-preservation measure in the face of shocking events that turn emotionally and psychologically threatening. In addition to the loss of a loved one and battlefield horrors, PTSD can be triggered by violent attacks, personally experienced or witnessed.

The assistance of a knowledgeable therapist is useful in guiding one through complicated grief and assessing the necessity of specialized help. Mental health centers and insurance providers can point the way to trauma therapy experts. Becoming aware of PTSD can help the mourner understand some of her or his struggles. These insights enhance patience. A therapist can offer direction if further help is required. The support of a professional can facilitate healing. The self-awareness garnered from working through the therapeutic process can lead to significant personal growth.

CHAPTER 14

Empathize

Helping Others

After one has recovered from grief, like it or not, he or she becomes an expert, someone others may lean on in their sorrow. Eventually everyone loses a loved one. When that happens, it is natural to offer help. Others may not know what to say or do. One who has been through grief can empathize. This person should resist superimposing her or his experience on the recent mourner. Circumstances differ from person to person. There are many ways to be of assistance to a mourner. Some approaches are significant sources of support. Others are counterproductive. It is important to know the difference.

Preparing to Be Helpful

To be helpful to a friend in grief requires preparation. It is common to feel helpless when seeking to comfort another. Most of us don't know what to do or say. A sense of dread may overcome good intentions, causing a friend to avoid helping or even visiting the mourner. This stems from uncertainty of what is appropriate. Hesitancy can bring resentment on the mourner's part, wondering why he or she hasn't heard from the reluctant friend.

The following suggestions can be helpful in knowing how to approach such delicate situations:

- A friend desiring to help should recall his own mourning experiences. He should remember who died and how it occurred. He should consider his reactions. He should give serious thought to how his friends attempted to comfort him. What was helpful? What was not?

It may be useful for the would-be supporter to trace his death experiences to his first significant loss, even dating back to childhood. Not only might this offer insight as to how one deals with death as an adult, but it will also enable deep empathy especially with one working through the process for the first time.

- The one wishing to be supportive should read as much as possible about the grieving process. This will provide the foundation for understanding the emotional blow being suffered by her friend.

  The more one knows about the grieving process, the better she is positioned to help. This stems from identifying with how the mourner is feeling. This also sheds light on whether the mourner should be advised to seek professional help.

- As a source of support, a friend should consider the totality of circumstances surrounding the death. The helping friend should factor how certain complications may be affecting mourning.

- It is hard to know the right words to say, but a good starting point is using correct language and avoiding euphemisms. One who has died is "dead," not "gone to a better place." This hints at denial.

The *Washington Post* published a special pullout section ("Every 28 Seconds," February 21, 2021) chronicling three of the deadliest days in the deadliest month of the coronavirus pandemic. In one vignette, a Pennsylvania County coroner, Scott Lynn, put it this way: "To start the grieving process, you basically have to hit 'em between the eyes."

Correct language is how a friend can say he or she understands the situation and accepts the reality of what has transpired. Mourners can slip into denial. Correct terminology keeps a friend from stumbling into fantasy.

When Death Arrives

The reality of death generally elicits either an intuitive or instrumental grieving style. A supportive friend should understand the difference.

For an intuitive griever, the experience is primarily emotional. Dealing with intense sadness takes place as an outward expression. Initial grief is characterized by low energy. Coping proceeds slowly. Adjustments are achieved through talking. For the friend wishing to help, active listening and connection are most helpful.

The experience is physical and cognitive for the instrumental griever. This person processes through tasks. This manifests as the mourner prioritizes funeral arrangements over attending to her or his own emotional needs. Anxiety is the hallmark of instrumental grieving. Coping progresses through problem solving. Comfort is found in routine. For this mourner, practical information and memorializing are most helpful.

Exquisite Witness

For anyone hoping to be helpful during another's bereavement, it is important to understand the role of exquisite witness. The idea is taught in volunteer trainings conducted by the Wendt Center for Loss and Healing. The Wendt Center has been a pillar of grief and trauma counseling in Washington, D.C., since the 1970s.

Defining the words establishes a framework that a supporter should keep in mind. "Exquisite" describes interaction centered in respect, care, honesty, and listening deeply from the perspective of the mourner. Such listening leads to understanding the mourner's anger and confusion. "Witness" acknowledges that the grief journey is the mourner's to own.

In *Helping Grieving People—When Tears Are Not Enough: A Handbook for Care Providers*, J. Shep Jeffreys explains that exquisite witnesses observe more than they act and listen more than they counsel. He advises that the witness's function is to follow rather than lead. This "mouth shut, ears open" technique honors the authority and dignity of the one in grief (Jeffreys, 8).

Jeffreys adds, "What distinguishes an exquisite witness is not one's level of training but one's willingness to approach another human being with compassion and deep respect for that person's needs, fear, and grief" (Jeffreys, 3). Jeffreys frames such sensitive interaction as witnessing with one's heart, head, and hands. The heart dominates as the helper's own unfinished grieving gets sparked by her or his role as supporter. A lack of awareness of one's own loss history means that he or she cannot be available to the mourner.

The head comes into play to comprehend grief, how it manifests and morphs. This knowledge lets the helper know what to expect. The exquisite helper's hands are involved in actions assisting in the mourning process. Those hands hold the grieving person and her or his grief.

Megan Devine expands on holding another's grief. She counsels that mourners don't need solutions, nor do they need to move on from their grief. What is needed is someone to see and acknowledge that grief. Devine adds that mourners do not need someone holding their hands while they stand in horror, gaping at the hole in their lives. She cautions that some things cannot be fixed, only carried.

Another distinction the caregiver should recognize is that between pain and suffering. Pain is the pure, raw emotion of loss. It is heart-based. Suffering is mental manipulations, mind games producing anxiety. The one providing comfort should be careful not to take away the mourner's pain. Such overprotection denies grief's reality and thwarts healing. Think of pain as proportional to the degree of love shared with the deceased. The mourner needs to go through, not around, the pain.

The supportive friend should focus on suffering, the symptoms of pain. Too little or too much sleep, a lack of exercise, an overdose of junk food, and an abuse of drugs or alcohol all can be adjusted in healthier directions. Caregivers can lessen suffering without blunting the pain.

A checklist for the helpful supporter may look like this:

1. Recognize the difference between pain and suffering in grief.

2. Acknowledge that grief's pain belongs to the mourner, not the helper.

3. Allow and bear witness to the pain. This is how one tends to it.

4. Validate the nature of the pain. It can feel like death just occurred.

5. Normalize symptoms of acute grief.

6. Realize that our culture inflicts additional suffering on top of grief.

The exquisite witness should bear in mind a few key points. Silence is a useful and natural part of being with someone. The quiet space between two individuals allows time to think, process, reflect, develop ideas, and relax. Relaxing in times of stress is not to be taken lightly.

Exquisite listening means listening more with our hearts than our minds. Such listening resists verbal responses. It trusts when verbalizing is not necessary. It emphasizes simply being present as a comforting tool.

Exquisite Witness as Excellent Grief Companion, Not Therapist

Often prescribed by religious mandate, the time between death and funeral is short. In the intervening period there is much to be done. Friends can assist with immediate tasks and those requiring planning.

Upon learning of the death, a friend should contact the survivor as soon as possible. Outreach may be done by phone, but a personal visit is better. It is a critical time when a friend in need most needs a friend. The bereaved may be unable to articulate emotions but will be looking for support and comfort. A trusted friend can become a guide who helps lead the mourner through sadness and gradually back to a normal life.

The first contact with one in deep grief will be awkward. Finding the right words is difficult. A sudden or violent death may elicit denial. Where to start? How to break the emotional ice? These are natural questions that run through the minds of those who would like to help.

Seeking validation of the death and clarification of the circumstances is a starting point. A friend might begin the conversation, sharing hope that the news of death is mistaken. A short follow-up—"Is this true?"—is in order. This opening allows the mourner to explain what happened. The supporter has an opportunity to let reality settle into her or his own thinking. This pause also accommodates the bereaved's need to review details as they wrestle with reality.

Listening attentively may be the best help a friend can give. Talking through one's pain is essential for recovery. Once the bereaved has described the situation, a simple "I'm sorry" will be comforting.

In the aftermath of death, many immediate tasks must be addressed. One person may not be able to manage everything. A friend taking the lead may organize and delegate duties among others. Assignments include the following:

- Making phone calls when this task exhausts the bereaved. Friends and relatives need to be informed so that travel arrangements may be made. The mourner should be consulted for wording he or she would like used.
- Helping make the mourner's house presentable. People may stop in to offer condolences and bring a meal. If the mourner is Jewish, the family may observe the ritual of sitting shiva, which anchors them at home for up to seven days. The bereaved may appreciate help organizing and tidying the house.
- Answering landlines. There may be incoming calls. Someone to receive and sort the messages is helpful. The mourner may wish to speak with some callers and prefer that others be handled by friends. The person handling phone calls should keep track of calls for future follow-up.
- Recording food delivered and dishes to be returned. When writing thank-you cards, the mourner will appreciate

knowing who brought what. Another helping hand may be required to sort delivered items, putting away some for later use and unwrapping other gifts for immediate consumption.

- Attending to routine errands. Doing even the simplest chores removes items from the mourner's worries. Walking the dog or grabbing groceries seem like little things. But such assistance lightens the bereaved's load. A friend might ask what needs to be done, organizing the errands and divvying up the assignments.
- Arranging accommodations for those visiting from afar. Brought together by the unfortunate circumstance of death, a supportive community of mourners can be fostered when out-of-towners are hosted by local friends and relatives.
- Providing transportation for out-of-town family and friends. Those traveling long distances to attend the funeral will appreciate a ride from the train terminal or airport to where they are staying.
- Making travel arrangements should the death require an out-of-town visit. Assistance might include a lift to the airport or the train station, retrieving the mail and the newspaper, monitoring deliveries, notifying an employer or teachers, and attending to other house-sitting duties.
- Encouraging the mourner to withdraw from earthly worries and rest.
- Assisting with the survivor's children. A loved one's death can be upsetting, even frightening, to children. Compounding the situation is the grief with which the parents must contend. They may be so caught up in their own raw emotions that they have little left to comfort their kids. A friend can help support grieving children.

Death from a Child's Point of View

Death is an unwelcome invader into a child's world. It may accompany the loss of a beloved pet or the death of a much-admired grandparent. Death impacts a child with a sibling's fatal accident or a parent's traumatic demise. Families coping with sorrow need to remember that children are impacted by the loss too. Their needs must be met.

Talking with children about death is not that much different than discussing other matters. Adults should be natural, trusting honest conversation. The adult should listen attentively. Being supportive is keeping open lines of communication. A reassuring touch also helps.

Questions to anticipate from a child curious about death and dying include the following:

What happens after you die?
What is heaven like?
Where do pets go?
Why are we buried?
Grandma died when I was little. I wasn't so sad then. I am now.
    Is that ok?
I went to my dad's funeral. Can he still see me?
What should I do if my brother or sister dies?

Tell the Truth

When discussing death with children, it is important to be honest. An adult should not make up stories to protect the child from the unpleasantness of loss. Phrases such as "Grandpa went on a long trip" and "Mommy is sleeping" should be avoided.

Conceptually, death is understood differently by children of different ages. The following are some basic ideas an adult might wish to raise:

When a person dies, his body stops functioning.
His heart stops beating.
He cannot eat, talk, or walk.
The dead person will not come back or visit anymore.
Nothing the child did or said caused the person to get sick or
    die.

Angel head on headstone, Bellefontaine Cemetery, St. Louis, Missouri (2020).

Mostly, people die when they are very old. Sometimes, people die before they are old. This may require a deeper conversation.

Soulful Discussion

Many faiths teach that all people possess a soul. This aspect of humans makes each unique and special, connecting each to the life force. The soul is the essence of human dignity. A religious perspective is that at the moment of birth, the soul attaches to the body. That body grows, ages, and eventually ceases to work and dies. When this happens, the soul is released from the body and rejoins the universe, perhaps to be returned to God's presence.

It may be helpful to explain that although the body is visible, the soul is not. Perhaps the soul is felt through prayer or thinking or dreaming. Children may find this reassuring. They are heartened to know that the deceased's soul is still a presence in some way. Even if adults aren't certain about their own belief in a soul, they can deliver this comforting concept to their child, introducing the idea with "Many people believe...."

Each Child Is Different

It is important to realize questions that children pose reflect their individuality. Children deserve responses suited to their personalities. There is no single correct way for children to react to death. Sometimes they will be extremely sad and cry accordingly. At other times, they will want to escape the situation and just have fun. Kids can appear cranky or angry. Or they simply may want to play with friends, laugh, or be silly.

A parent should be available to talk with his children when they are ready to have a conversation. Parents might read books to their kids to open the discussion. Parents also should allow their children the freedom not to talk about death when they need the space. It is natural for children to worry about how the death will affect them. If a grandparent dies, they may worry about who will be next. If a parent dies, the concern for children will be who will be there to take care of them.

Children may become preoccupied with thoughts of disease if death resulted from illness or thoughts about accidents if this was the cause of death. Another concern that children may have is that they will be asked to fill the family role of the deceased. A supportive adult should be patient, answering questions honestly and in an age-appropriate manner.

Involving Children in the Mourning Process

Attitudes have changed toward involving children in mourning rituals. Overprotection was the prevailing approach for generations. Adults who grew up with disappointing memories of exclusion from consideration following a death in the family have ushered in new thinking.

Lessons drawn from these experiences indicate that children want to be included in the healing activities that constitute the traditions around death and mourning. These activities are healing for children too. Most children, with adequate preparation, can be taken to the funeral and burial of a loved one. It is their opportunity to say goodbye. An adult friend or relative should stand watch over each child, taking the child out for breaks if needed. Older children may be offered the chance to speak at the funeral. They could tell a story, sing a song, or recite a poem.

During the days following the funeral, children can be active participants in mourning rituals rather than be problems to be avoided. During the mourning period, children can be introduced to the idea of comforting someone after a death. A child with a friend who has lost a loved one can be taught about dealing with death. Adults may accompany their child on a visit to the friend's home and model appropriate behavior. Parents can teach their child how to give a hug and talk about the deceased. Parents, along with their child, might deliver food to demonstrate how friends provide sustenance and caring.

Healing Through Remembering

Many traditions teach that the bereaved can help themselves in the healing process through active remembering. Mourners can reflect by having photos of the deceased placed around the house and by relating stories about their loved one. Helpful activities for children include creating a scrapbook about the deceased and constructing a family tree that features both living and deceased family members.

Common practices include charitable donations in the deceased's name. Children may relate to planting a tree in the deceased's memory or doing acts of kindness such as those performed by their loved one.

Heed the Stewardess's Advice

When safety measures are explained to passengers before an airplane takes off, one directive is for parents traveling with small children to put their oxygen masks on before attending to their kids. The same principle applies to adults dealing with a death in the family.

Adult mourners must meet their own needs first in order to be of assistance to their kids.

Hard as it may be, parents should try to get adequate sleep and eat well. Parents should try to surround themselves with people who understand their trauma and can empathize with their grief. Parents should make sure that they have wise counsel available and professional help to call on should the situation warrant for themselves or their children.

Parents who are in mourning may wish to ask friends to assist with their children. Other parents can be of service driving carpools and helping with homework. Although children certainly will need their parents' attention through the difficult days following a loved one's death, both parent and child may benefit from time spent playing with other neighborhood kids.

It is important for grieving parents to allow others to help them. In the future, the bereaved may have an opportunity to return the favor. That is what it means to live in community.

Children Becoming Resilient

As children will learn, death is part of life. They may be stronger than their parents think. They are tough and will survive. Children will be able to use this difficult time to absorb valuable life lessons.

Children will learn how to be resilient. They will learn how to rely on others for caring and how to offer comfort to those they love. They will learn how to participate in their tradition's teachings about healing from the trauma of death. Children will learn that life is to be enjoyed to the fullest. They will realize that this is the antidote to the sadness of death.

PART III

Pivoting to Support Others

CHAPTER 15

Heart Work

It is good for a friend to know that even for counseling professionals, grief work is a curiosity-based therapy. The subtitle of Megan Devine's work *It's OK That You're Not OK* speaks volumes: *Meeting Grief and Loss in a Culture That Doesn't Understand.* Not imposing one's beliefs on the bereaved is an important principle. Being open to the mourner's experiences and emotions is key to understanding. Empathic listening lets the mourner know that someone cares, someone is trying to understand.

A brief personal aside takes me back to my father's death. As I was delivering his eulogy from prepared notes, three words came to me that I hadn't placed on the page: "He understood understanding." His life's work was devoted to interfaith community relations. Understanding others was integral to his personal and professional life. Where the words came from at that moment I do not know. I stumbled onto the perfect tribute. When my mother and brother heard the phrase, they were certain that those words should be chiseled on his headstone.

Seeking to understand others reveals cross-cultural considerations that enhance exquisite witnessing. To riff off Megan Devine's title, it's okay for a supportive friend not to know, not to have all the answers. Such honesty leads to cultural humility.

R.M. Ortega and K.C. Faller speak to this in their manual *Training Child Welfare Workers from an Intersectional Cultural Humility Perspective: A Paradigm Shift.* "Demonstrating cultural humility frees workers from having to possess expert knowledge about an array of cultural differences" (Ortega and Faller, 27). The authors emphasize that the advantage of this perspective is that it positions the worker "in a learning mode" rather than "maintaining control in the working relationship." This is particularly useful regarding "cultural experiences about which the client is far more knowledgeable."

When the exquisite witness yields to cultural humility, diversity's complexity is embraced. Self-awareness is fostered. Learning and curiosity are encouraged. Cultural differences are more easily accepted. Cultural humility sparks collaborative learning and deeper understanding of the emotional environment. It challenges structural inequalities.

Culture humility leads with sincere curiosity and might ask these questions:

- What was the experience like for you?
- Would you care to tell me more about that?
- Which aspect of your identity do you believe this touches?
- Is there family history impacting your interaction today?
- I'm not familiar with that custom/tradition/practice. Would you like to tell me more about that?
- What are the ways your family has honored your loved one?

Emotional Support

Reverberating through these pages is the idea that one of life's most demanding passages is dealing with the loss of a loved one. Time seems frozen. Sadness stretches into the unforeseeable future. Coping with simple daily matters is exhausting. Decisions stemming from a loved one's death can be daunting. The existential questions can be draining when one wonders what it means to one's life now that a significant connection to the past has been buried.

During such times a mourner will find priceless those friends who listen, reflect, share the pain, and assist in the grieving process. Being there in a thoughtful, meaningful way at the moments of deepest sorrow is perhaps the greatest service a friend can perform. Compassion and concern are the critical components necessary for a friend to come through. It is a tall order to provide support during such trying times. But here are some communication keys:

- The supportive friend should let the mourner know she is available whenever the bereaved is ready to talk. When this offer is made, the friend should be prepared for an instant response. This invitation could be exactly what the mourner needed to open up.

  Alternatively, the mourner may not feel that is the right moment to speak but will know that a concerned listener is ready when he is.

- As the mourner opens up, a friend should ask questions requiring more than yes or no answers. The mourner will know that the listener's interest is genuine. This encourages the mourner to engage thoughtfully. These questions keep the mourner talking.

- Conversation prompts can keep the mourner engaged. Interjecting comments such as "Yes, I see" and "Then what happened?" will reassure the mourner that she is being heard.

- Nonverbal communication cues should be used. Eye contact, leaning in, nodding, appropriate touching, and facial responses let the speaker know the listener is plugged into the conversation.

- The importance of using correct language cannot be overstated. This includes avoiding euphemisms. Fuzzy terms such as "passed away" and "in a better place" may seem like they take the edge off a difficult situation when in fact they encourage denial.

  There are exceptions. If the bereaved is still in shock and cannot bear to hear words such as "murder" and "suicide" so soon after the death, a friend should consider his relationship with the mourner and how they've communicated difficult topics in the past. If the friend feels this is not the time for blunt talk, harsh honesty may need to be tamped down. Experience is the guide to handle this situation.

- If the supporter also knew the deceased, sharing memories may be comforting. This can be very welcome if the deceased went through a life transformation at some distance from the mourner.

A visit from army buddies or college friends can be heartwarming to the parents of a young adult child who died far from home. Grieving individuals may crave stories that bring loved ones back to life. Sharing happy memories may be mutually beneficial in the grieving process of both the listener and the storyteller.

- Reflective listening helps mourners solve issues. Restating a problem with well-articulated alternatives can shed light on solutions.
- Help can come in the form of prioritizing the day's activities. What should be tackled first? What can wait?
- Time and patience are important gifts that a friend may offer the bereaved. If the mourner needs to cry, he should be allowed to do so. This can be an essential element of the process.

  The friend needn't do more than keep quiet company. A hug, a shawl, and a cup of tea are nonverbal symbols of warmth and caring. If the mourner needs to vent, a friend who simply listens to the anger can aid in emotional release. This often lifts the mourner's mood.
- A good listener is golden. Friends may feel awkward just listening. People can feel pressure to say the right thing, to utter something that magically makes everything better. Such moments sometimes scream out for silence.

  A quiet, calming presence can be the proper elixir in difficult settings. Letting the mourner speak her or his mind often is the best thing a friend can do to be supportive. Release and relief can come from these nonverbal exchanges. A mourner will appreciate the chance to talk about his sorrow to someone who is truly attentive and doesn't interrupt or offer shallow encouragement to buck up.
- If the would-be supporter senses he has confused the mourner or thinks the mourner is not really listening, the friend might pose a question to make sure he is being properly received. It is good to confirm that messages are being accurately processed.

To guard against misunderstanding, a mourner may be asked to paraphrase what he has heard. One is not seeking mindless parroting of previous statements. Rather, by putting in his own words what he thinks has been said, a meeting of the minds can be reached. Paraphrasing helps achieve accurate communication. To be useful, messages must be clearly interpreted.

CHAPTER 16

Lessons Learned from Professionals

Hospice Workers

Those who engage in end-of-life hospice care—doctors, nurses, social workers, volunteers—have much to teach mourners and those who soon will be bereaved. There are few fields so immersed in death and dying. These professionals have heard all the usual questions: Why would anyone choose to do hospice work? Why would someone opt to spend their career so deeply entangled with dying-induced grief? How is it possible to get up the next morning and do it all over again?

As intense and exhausting as the work is, one rarely hears hospice professionals complain that their jobs are disheartening. Rather, they're likely to describe their work as fulfilling. It may seem counterintuitive, but "life-affirming" often is used to explain what they do. Annual turnover rates at hospice facilities are surprisingly low. Hospice centers are wary of employee burnout and are on guard against "compassion fatigue." With more Americans choosing hospice care, maintaining a dedicated, rejuvenated workforce is a constant concern. According to a report from the Medicare Payment Advisory Commission, the number of hospice patients grew 167 percent, to more than 1.4 million, between 2000 and 2016. Nearly half the Medicare beneficiaries who died in 2015 availed themselves of hospice services.

By standard medical measures, hospice doctors might be considered failures. Depending on the size of their facility, such personnel could lose up to two dozen patients a week. But those who work in hospice care do not assess themselves by the binary metrics of life or death. In their professional capacities, death is constant, unavoidable, inevitable.

While they know there is little they can fix at the end of life, hospice professionals are sustained by the belief that their work is sacred. These caregivers evaluate their performance by how well they guide their patients to their end. They know that the most they can do is give their patients an opportunity to have the best deaths possible. That may mean a pain-free death and for the fortunate a death free of distress. While most people run away from death, hospice workers rush toward it. They carry with them the knowledge that they know what their patients are going through and the attitude that they are there to help.

There is a shortage of hospice care in the United States. There are too few doctors and nurses to keep up with an aging population, especially in rural areas. Many facilities are understaffed, particularly those providing home care. It is not unusual for a hospice center to conduct extensive fundraising to supplement Medicare to be able to offer additional services such as music and art therapy.

The easier task for a hospice professional is relieving a patient's physical symptoms. Medication can control pain and agitation. Much of death, however, is not medical. Many in the field believe that their more daunting challenges are spiritual and psychological. Hospice workers know they cannot smooth over all slights or eliminate all resentments. But often they do try to facilitate discussions that result in deathbed reconciliations.

The prevailing attitude of hospice care providers seems to be that they get more from their work than they give, and they give a lot. It is thought that the work is a way for them to sync their soul with their role. Common takeaways for those engaged in this work are learning not to hold onto resentments and making the extra effort to find joy in the everyday.

Knowing they can positively influence the end of their patients' lives carries care workers forward. They lean into the challenges, knowing that their presence makes a difference. They hold their patients' hands with a sense of honor. The hospice worker helps the patient find peace and comfort and in so doing upholds the dignity of that patient's life. All the while, the hospice professional may be learning not to fear death.

Hospice workers may or may not be religiously observant but generally think of themselves as spiritually inclined. The job may confirm one's faith while challenging one's beliefs. This is especially so when a caregiver witnesses a patient suffering. That's when the work requires something extra, be that prayer or meditation or nature.

Those in the field need to be intentional about self-care. They must find ways to replenish themselves to stay mentally engaged in their work. It is critical that care providers not suppress their feelings. It is important that they develop ways to process and share their emotions with others. A primary risk is compassion fatigue, numbing to the suffering of others. This is a sensation that caregivers may experience. The indicators are increased irritability, dread of going to work, and inability to experience joy. Malaise can be accompanied by substance abuse. Characteristic of compassion fatigue is use of depersonalized language as when a care worker refers to a patient by diagnosis instead of name.

Coping mechanisms caregivers use include yoga, stretching, and other stress-reducing exercises. Hospice employees are encouraged to find peers in whom they can confide. Staff often develop their own activities to acknowledge the meaning of their work, such as ceremonies to honor the lives and memories of their patients.

Death Doulas

Another model for mourners is that of death doulas. Some prefer the terms "end-of-life doulas," "soul midwives," or "transition coaches." Whatever they are called, these people provide a quiet, comforting presence at the end of life. They stand sentry, easing passage from this world to the next.

The doula understands that his company is the most valuable assistance he can offer anyone undertaking that most solitary journey. The doula sits silently, wishing the soon-to-be-departed peace and comfort. One technique of the experienced doula is slipping her hand under her patient's, palm to palm, rather than resting her hand on top. This is helpful with patients who can no longer speak, enabling them to express whether the touch is wanted by returning the grip.

The death doula field is attracting more professionals and volunteers. Like the childbirth doulas from which their name derives, the death doula's mission is to assist and accompany. Their patients' experience is as sacred as the birthing process although quieter and more sorrowful.

As the baby boomer generation transitions to retirement, aging is being reimagined along with treatment measures for the dying. Palliative caregivers acknowledge that pain management is not enough. They recognize that the spirit also must be attended to. The soon-to-be-bereaved should be included in the scope of care as well. From these realizations, death doulas are emerging. Those who engage in this work feel a compulsion to do it. They are profoundly moved by it. They want to be of service to others in a way that makes the final transition a better experience.

The training to become certified in the field covers the best ways to touch a dying person and when aromatherapy or guided visualizations might be helpful. Care extends to the dying individual's loved ones. A doula learns strategies to relieve overburdened family members and how to organize a legacy project to memorialize a patient's life.

The trained doula becomes versed in assisting both the dying and her or his dear ones at the moment of death. The doula's role extends to helping loved ones process grief in the ensuing weeks. To gain essential empathy, students training to become doulas reflect deeply on deaths that affected them. Instructors may ask aspiring doulas to recall how a significant death looked, smelled, and felt. Students dwell on how that experience shaped their definition of a "good death."

Doulas make the effort to transform their personal losses into something that could assist dying patients and their families. By revisiting their anguish and despair, doulas draw strength that helps them be more present when others are experiencing those sad, scary sensations.

Doulas fill many functions. Sometimes patients need assistance with physical care. At other times, families need help with household chores or errands. Whatever the need, it is the doula's job to listen. Doulas do so without judgment. They do so in a way that respects the experience of both the dying and their loved ones. Doulas facilitate interaction between the dying individual and her or his loved ones and encourage people to express everything they need to say. The soon-to-be mourners should have no regrets.

Often patients reach a point where they can no longer communicate verbally. The doula simply sits quietly, meditating and sending good wishes. The doula lets her patient know he is not alone. He is safe.

For doulas, the work can have the tangential effect of moving awareness of one's own mortality to the forefront of the mind. This can result in an even more profound appreciation for every day of life.

CHAPTER 17

Taking Care to Care for the Caregiver

While one is assisting a friend, the helper can lose sight of her own peace of mind. Exerting energy in support of another is exhausting. Attentive listening is hard work. Note the physical sensation of focused listening: sweaty palms, faster heart rate. It feels like a workout.

Absorbing the suffering of another is even harder. The one who gets to express himself may feel better, while the listener may feel drained. The supportive, active listener should take time to address her own needs. Being someone else's shoulder to lean on can sap one's strength. When the listener is still coping with her own loss, it may be too much to take on someone else's burden. The listener in this situation winds up doing less good for her friend and herself.

It is better to take a break and recharge one's batteries before resuming an intense listening session. The listener might offer to locate another sympathetic friend to share some of the weight. Being upfront with the mourner and explaining one's honest exhaustion should suffice to send a caring signal but one that also says that a little caregiver relief is needed.

What to Avoid

The best intentions may be misperceived. This can result in friction when uplift was intended. It's nice to be nice, but it is nicer to be clear. When emotions run high and nerves are wracked, it is important that messages are accurately received. Avoid these communication missteps:

175

- Empty platitudes:

"She's in a better place now."
"He's with Grandpa again."
"I feel your pain."
"Don't question what happened. It's part of a bigger plan."
"Count your blessings."
"Time to put this behind you and move on."
"You have so much to live for."
"Let me know if there's anything I can do."

These comments ring hollow, leaving a listener confused and frustrated.

Lighthearted caution concerning euphemisms comes from comedian Laurie Kilmartin. In the aftermath of her father's death, Kilmartin wrote *Dead People Suck: A Guide for Survivors of the Newly Departed*. The tongue-in-cheek text surely provided the author needed relief. One insight she offers is "I'm a big believer in the word *dead*. It is direct and clear" (Kilmartin, 155). Then, she admits that an argument can be made for euphemisms, especially in the early stages of grief. *"Passed away* is particularly gentle. When you say it, most adults will instinctively know that *dead* isn't part of your vocabulary yet."

Kilmartin points out a pitfall of being imprecise with kids:

"What does 'passed away' mean?"
"Well, it means Grandpa was called home."
"He's home? But I thought he was dead!"

The comedy writer notes that a six-year-old can bring you right back to square one, "face-to-face with that word you hate."

- Monopolizing the discussion. Speaking can provide emotional release. It is natural for those needing to vent to take command of the conversation. If trying to help, however, it is counterproductive to overwhelm a mourner with another's thoughts. If this is what's happening, one should pause and regain control of the impulse to talk. The bereaved should be encouraged to speak up.

A supportive friend will focus on what the mourner has to say without being judgmental. Empathetic understanding is key. If the helper finds himself anticipating what he will say next, composing his response in his head, he should clear his mind and return his concentration squarely on the one in need.

- "You should" statements. Starting a sentence that way implies superior knowledge. It can leave the impression the mourner isn't capable of making her own decisions or handling her own affairs.

  Those in grief can be inundated with advice. When enough suggestions are thrown one's way, there are bound to be contradictory directives. Rather than being helped, it is likely that the mourner will wind up confused and further frustrated.

  One wanting to help might be more reflective in his responses. Resisting "you should" and replacing that with "Have you given thought to ..." or "What do you want to do about..." empowers the mourner to engage fully in her own decision-making.

  When someone loses a loved one, there is a significant sense that one's own life is out of control. Restoring a modicum of control is movement in the right direction.

- Making the mourner's decisions for him. This begs for friendship insurance. The person who makes decisions on the mourner's behalf may well be blamed for anything that goes wrong. This can turn into a case of good intentions backfiring.

  A friend can be most supportive if she lays out options and lets the bereaved make his own decision. It may be hard for the friend to stay quiet if she disagrees, but this is a better way to proceed.

- Suppressing the mourner's emotions and discouraging expressions of grief. A good listener will not change the subject when the bereaved needs to talk.

  If the friend is ill at ease with what's being expressed, he might seek a substitute listener. No one can be expected to be good at all aspects of support. Better to find someone equipped to listen to difficult emotions. If another in the circle of friends cannot handle the conversation, a clergy person or therapist may be appropriate.

- Superimposing someone else's belief system. For instance, if the mourner does not believe in an afterlife, this is not the time to bring up such ideas. Being an objective, nonjudgmental listener accepting of the mourner's values is the support most needed.
- Coming across as an authority on grief. Everyone's life experiences are unique. What is true for one may not be the case for another.

  A supporter should not predict what the next stage of grief holds. Even one well read on grief who has given it great thought must remember the idiosyncrasies of each individual's circumstances.
- Encouraging the mourner to be dependent on a particularly strong friend. Even though that supporter may be helpful, the bereaved should be given the opportunity for personal growth afforded by grief.
- Dominating the bereaved's time and attention. A good friend should be considerate of the mourner's needs and of those in the circle of friends. There may be others who want to be helpful. They should not be deprived of the opportunity to nourish friendships.

  A sensitivity to when the mourner may want to be alone or to spend time with others will be appreciated. It also may be reenergizing for members of the inner circle to take an occasional break and share the responsibilities of support.

Extended Help

A bereaved friend may need care for some time to come. He may need a shoulder to lean on even more when supporters depart for home following the funeral. As others resume routines, the reality of loss may just start sinking in. The need for a sounding board may grow greater.

Friends should pace themselves. Following a death, others may charge ahead to attend to the many tasks, only to recognize that they cannot keep up such a schedule. They exhaust themselves and upset their families because they are gone for long stretches. This can be where friendships fray. Unable to maintain the pace, they pull back. The mourner can become confused and bitter, and an important relationship fades.

To prevent this, a friend must realize that one in mourning has much processing to do and that it may take months or years to resolve the grief. A good friend should determine how much he reasonably can give. The helping hand must pace herself so that time and energy are held in reserve to be able to lend assistance for as long as needed.

A visiting schedule may be beneficial to both the mourner and the helper. This could be weekly in the early goings and then stretched to every other week as time unfolds. The mourner will appreciate knowing she can rely on her friend to be there on certain days.

Postfuneral thank-you cards can be overwhelming. If the bereaved is feeling pressure, a friend can draft notes at the mourner's direction. Perhaps the mourner would like to visit the gravesite and would like some company. This is a helpful role a friend might play.

Another useful service a friend might supply is scouring beneficial community resources. There may be support groups, lectures or seminars that could provide uplift. The bereaved might like company at one of these informative events. This is another supportive action a good friend might take. Seeking the availability of specialized grief counselors also can be very useful.

CHAPTER 18

A Final Thought on Final Thoughts: An Ethical Will Is a Legacy of Love

In anticipation of one's own death, a powerful action that can be taken is drafting an ethical will. Such spiritual documents are windows into the authors' souls. An ethical will bequeaths values, not valuables. These "legacy letters" convey the most important messages the writer wants loved ones to know. They become a prized part of family history.

In Jewish tradition, an ethical will is a statement of personal values brimming with wisdom and aspirationally launched. Unlike a legal will, which directs distribution of assets, and a living will, which instructs next of kin how to deal with one's body, ethical wills have developed over centuries to bequeath life lessons with the desire that they be followed. Writing this will is almost instinctive. There seems to be an impulse that drives one to leave important messages for loved ones. There are many ways to draft ethical wills. Tone and style are at the writer's discretion.

Like any writing assignment, getting started can be the hardest part. To break writers' block requires rising above apprehension of being judged. A way to do this is to write as though the only reader is the writer. This lifts the restraints of others' judgments. Writing in "Dear Diary" style removes inhibitions of others' opinions, allowing free-flowing thought.

A few prompts can help writers zero in on pertinent topics:

What were the formative events in your life?
What was the world like when you were a child?

Pinpointing the important lessons in your life, what have you
learned that's worth passing along?

Who were the most influential figures in your life?

What were the causes you felt most deeply about?

What books meant the most to you?

What are your most prized possessions—tangible and
otherwise—and what stories are attached to these items?

What are your deepest regrets?

What is your definition of success? Has that changed over time?

How does reviewing your life make you feel?

If you were to seek or grant another's forgiveness, what would
that be about?

What is your basis of appreciation for readers of this ethical
will?

Outlining one's thoughts helps the flow of ideas. Once topics have
been selected, the writer can use each heading to start a separate
section.

Each topic deserves its own page. Each question/statement
becomes a topic sentence to be developed into supporting paragraphs. Some of the topics may spill over into subsequent passages. If
so, pages on the same subject should be attached.

The pages of each subject may be considered a separate section. They may be arranged and rearranged until the writer has them
in the desired order. Such sequencing could be chronological, geo-
graphical, in any order important to the writer. All passages should
be proofread with an eye toward keeping the flow coherent. After
the initial draft, the writer may wish to edit, correct, and rewrite as
needed. Letting the document marinate awhile allows the author to
return to the manuscript with fresh eyes before proceeding.

The next challenge for the writer is to personalize the piece. A
good way to do this is to include buzz words, favorite expressions
and anecdotes that have special meaning to the author's family.
An example is the tone and delivery of one of my mother's favorite phrases. She would tenderly grasp the hands of one of her sons,
daughters-in-law, or grandkids and fix a faux stern gaze into their

eyes. In a mock demanding voice, as if barking critical instructions, she would say, "I love you! DO YOU UNDERSTAND?!" This silly expression of affection continues to resonate with her family years after her death.

Most ethical wills are prepared as written text, though they may be recorded in audio or video format. Since advances in technology can render electronic documentation obsolete and since whatever's recorded generally starts as a script, the written word remains the favored medium for ethical wills. Documentation on high-quality stationery is long-lasting, readily reproduced, and suitable for framing.

The proper time for conveyance of an ethical will is subject to individual choice. Some prefer to deliver it shortly after it is written. Others would rather review and revise it over time if life's circumstances permit. Some writers decide that this spiritual document should not be read until after their death, as a codicil to their material will. Others choose to do both, presenting one will while alive and a second loving codicil later. However the document is delivered, it should be reviewed and updated periodically during the grantor's lifetime.

There are a few other considerations before turning the page on ethical wills. Those who have drafted a living will should inform their children about what it contains and where it is to be found. Decisions about organ donation and cremation may be discussed with clergy and with mature children.

The distribution of material goods as directed in one's will is another matter one may wish to explain to heirs. This is an appropriate time to resolve unfinished business that otherwise would be left dangling with survivors. It is good to take advantage of a last chance to make peace.

Dignity Therapy Can Be Uplifting at the End of Life

In the mid–1990s, psychiatrist Harvey Chochinov and his team studied depression in patients nearing death. The research was driven by a key question: Why do some dying individuals wish for death and consider suicide, while others, experiencing similar symptoms, feel a serene will to live to their final days?

In the following decade, Chochinov and his colleagues at the University of Manitoba in Canada created a therapy intended to reduce anxiety, the urge to die, and suicidal thoughts at the end of life. It is known as dignity therapy and features guided conversation with a trained therapist, enabling dying people to talk about what matters most to them. It is conversation that invites people to speak their mind before they are no longer able to do so.

Dignity therapy may not be well known to the general public, but it has captured the attention of end-of-life researchers around the globe. Studies have not yet concluded specific benefits, but analysis does confirm that patients, families, and clinicians heartily approve.

End-of-life discussions are significant. A critical need of those who are aware they are dying is taking care of relationships with individuals who matter to them. This includes expressing their wishes to family and ensuring that loved ones can say goodbye without regret.

The closer people get to death, the more they need to know their lives counted for something. However defined, they need to know that their lives had importance and were valued by others. Dignity therapy addresses the need to find meaning in life. It does so in a structured, effective way.

PART IV

How Various Cultures Comfort Their Mourners

My mother's death left me an orphan at the age of 58. While I felt fortunate to have at least one parent for that much of my life, I still was devastated by the loss. A cousin gave me a book that explained the Jewish rituals I was observing. I found comfort as I melted into the pages of Anita Diamant's *Saying Kaddish*. Relying on rituals might be considered an emotional crutch. But when one's heart is broken—just as when one hobbles around on a broken leg—a crutch is exactly what is needed. It is in this spirit that I offer the following chapters.

I am not an anthropologist, but ever since mourning my mother I have been interested in how other cultures comfort the bereaved. As a university professor of communication, I encounter colleagues and students from across the globe. I have discussed with several the rituals from their homelands. Some of my students were quite familiar with the mourning customs of their countries. For others it was an intriguing challenge to learn more about this aspect of their culture. I have interwoven their stories throughout this text.

What follows is a broad cross-representation of ethnicities, a collection of some of the most interesting research upon which I compiled *We Who Grieve*. I hope mourners and those who care about them can find contemplation and comfort in these insights.

CHAPTER 19

Indigenous Australians: Humankind's Original Instincts

Long before Australia was colonized by the British in the late eighteenth century, the continent was home to a civilization considered one of the oldest continuous cultures on Earth, the indigenous Australian. It is believed that these people migrated from Africa 50,000 years ago.

Several hundred indigenous communities still exist across the continent, totaling nearly half a million people. Many scholars believe that indigenous Australian traditions represent some of the oldest known to man. Studying their rituals is one of the truest forms of anthropology. Limited research exists on ancient native traditions around death and funerals. Recent studies examine the roots of those traditions based on current practices. Although deaths attributed to causes other than old age were rare, settlers' introduction of disease and lifestyle changes worsened death rates among young and middle-aged adults.

Contemporary indigenous groups have adapted mourning rituals in many ways to maintain their values of community support and ancestral connection in the face of death. Their unique customs serve as a reassertion of independence from Western influence and a way to express control over their lives in an ever-changing world. The native belief system is referred to as "Dreamtime" and "The Dreaming." These terms, loosely translated by settlers in the late nineteenth century, describe Earth's creation and the continuing relationship between the living, their ancestors, and nature.

Australia's indigenous believe that the Earth was created by their ancestors through rituals of song and dance that formed the land and sea and its inhabitants. Their beliefs are rooted in respect for ancestors and the natural world. Songs and dance performances are important aspects of all rituals, particularly ones in which the dead join their ancestral line. Because deaths prior to old age now occur so frequently, mourning is an accepted part of life. Funerals have become the most common ritual performed in indigenous communities.

Immediate and continuous support for those grieving a loss is one of the community's most critical shared values. News of a death is received with urgency. Work is stopped. Other rituals may be postponed for weeks. It is considered disrespectful to engage in mundane behaviors until proper rituals are performed and the deceased is buried. Attendance of the entire community is expected to ensure full support for the grieving family. Altogether, the rituals represent much more than occasions to mourn a loss; they are also intended to reaffirm relationships among families and strengthen connections to ancestors.

Preparations Before and After Death

Little information exists on how Australia's indigenous prepare for death. Some communities believe that unusual events or a pain in specific parts of the body may be omens that a death has occurred or is imminent.

For the dying, it is common to gather close family members nearby. At the moment of death, the person may make the sign of her or his clan and ask that ancestral songs be performed. Such songs are specific to certain clans and are an important aspect of mourning and funeral ceremonies.

After a death, the message circulates to extended family and others who knew the deceased. People with ties to the deceased or her or his family may travel great distances to attend the funeral and support the relatives. To accommodate the time required to cover vast distances, burials are rarely held sooner than three weeks after death. This enables family members and friends to be present. If circumstances prevent attending, it is expected that supporters send messages to be read at the funeral. Communities question the loyalty of those who do not offer support. Failure to act is perceived as denying one's relationship to the deceased.

The term "bad news" is frequently reserved in Australia for the delivery of a death notice. Name suppression is a tradition followed by nearly all indigenous communities. The deceased's name is not uttered. To avoid any reference the message is phrased "Bad news from [community], [name of family] doesn't have a [relation of deceased]." While name suppression may seem an unhealthy denial, it is an ongoing reminder of the family's loss. Because it is obvious that the name is being avoided, the practice serves to acknowledge the deceased and the impact of the loss on the community.

Another common postdeath practice in indigenous communities is abandoning the place where the deceased lived, even to the extent of walking down a different street to avoid the former residence. Because structures are now built more permanently, family members may switch houses with distant kin in order to adhere to this practice. Such efforts are meant to limit potential interaction with the deceased's spirit, considered most dangerous the first two days after death. The spirit is believed to be lonely and jealous of living relatives and may act out violently. The spirit also may watch family members to ensure they perform mourning rituals, bringing harm to those who fail to do so.

Some communities may "warm" the house by performing a smoke ceremony to rid the place of the deceased's spirit and encourage it to let go of worldly attachments. The windows and doors may be left open, and community members will stand watch for indications that the spirit has left.

As the deceased's house is abandoned, so too are his possessions. Hanging on to belongings poses another risk to the living of interacting with the spirit. Smaller items are burned or buried with the deceased, while more expensive possessions are given away to distant relatives.

Community Reactions to Death

Communal support following a death is expected in indigenous communities. It is common for close relatives, particularly women, to wail as a public expression of grief. Others will embrace mourners and sob with them even if they were not personally affected by the death.

Despite name suppression, the Wiradjuris in central New South Wales talk extensively about the deceased in death's aftermath. Community members believe that such discussions help mourners focus on the deceased rather than obsessing on themselves. They believe that the greatest loss is failing to recall the deceased and her or his contributions to the community.

The deceased's loved ones may cut their hair to identify themselves as in grief. In extreme cases, close family may inflict wounds on themselves as manifestations of their pain. Others usually try to prevent this. The discomfort felt by Westerners unaccustomed to such public and sometimes violent displays of grief has limited many of these practices. Some communities, such as the Murris of Charters Towers in northern Queensland, conform to Western beliefs by restricting their condolences to a simple touch and "I'm sorry." Although excessive reactions to death may be perceived as insincere, they can be a significant aspect of the grieving process. They express an appreciation of the suffering experienced by those in mourning.

One unfortunate but common response to a death is disputes over its cause. Since the indigenous now rarely die of old age, it is believed that human factors must have contributed to the death. Family members may feel angry and seek to blame those they feel contributed to the death. Male family members take the lead in making public displays of anger. They may even attempt to avenge the death. While acts of anger may appear unhealthy, they serve as an opportunity for the community to vent grievances. They also give the community a chance to settle differences in order to make peace in light of the loss.

Most communities refer to the practices and rituals surrounding death as "sorry business." This reflects the importance of expressing sadness about the death and condolences for all those affected. Although not all communities use the same terminology, they usually perform similar rituals. Since premature death has become a much more common occurrence, sorry camps, funerals, and reburial ceremonies are established aspects of indigenous culture.

Sorry Camps

After a death, close mourners hold "sorry meetings" or move into sorry camps to begin receiving friends and relatives who have traveled to offer condolences. Key mourners include the spouse, parents, and siblings and their spouses. They stay in one part of the camp, separated by gender. Such separation may be maintained throughout the grieving process. The deceased's body may rest in this part of the sorry camp.

Staying at the camp isolates mourners from the community and signals certain restrictions such as refraining from meat. For the spouse, abstaining from sexual relations or remarriage is part of this grieving phase. Traditionally, the entire community observes the mourning period for two to three weeks during which personal interactions are subdued and quiet is generally maintained.

Warlpiri communities in the Tanami Desert gather at sorry camps by organizing into four quadrants: first divided by gender, then by key mourners and those who have arrived to offer condolences. White ochre is applied to mourners' temples and upper torso in different shapes for men and women. The ochre is different than what is used in other rituals. It is duller and applied less precisely than the pleasing designs used on more celebratory occasions.

On the male and female sides, attendees approach mourners in a specific style of dance while carrying boomerangs or other weapons. Men may sing, while woman sing and cry. The songs differ in tone, rhythm, and pitch. Everyone has a role to play in the songs even if it is just listening and watching the performance. The songs build a sense of community and help "sing" the deceased along their spiritual journey to join ancestors (Magowan, 83). Once the groups reach

each other, attendees kneel in front of mourners, touch them, and join in their sobs and wails. The most prominent mourner, usually the parent or spouse, may have in front of them a bedroll that represents the deceased and contains a lock of her or his hair.

After all attendees have offered condolences, the quadrants dissolve, and male family members of the deceased move to the middle of the camp. The brothers of the deceased's mother are encouraged to avenge the death. A fight might erupt if certain attendees or their relatives are believed to have contributed to the death. Fights may subside as attendees depart the camp or continue throughout the sorry period (Venbrux, 89). Female mourners often cry loudly at night as the camp is sleeping. Other women join in to show support. The wailing continues until close mourners go back to sleep. Mourners are not to feel alone in their grief.

These daily and nightly rituals are repeated as more attendees arrive. The size of the sorry camp and its duration vary based on the deceased's age and status in the community. Key mourners may stay at the camp for weeks or even months in extreme cases.

After the last sorry meeting, the bedroll is unrolled and the lock of hair is passed around to be touched by everyone. The oldest brother of the deceased's mother keeps the lock of hair as a reminder to avenge the death. The rituals performed at sorry camps traditionally were separate from the funeral. It has become common to merge the ceremonies.

Funeral Practices

Traditionally, relatives from the deceased's generation are responsible for final preparations after death. They tend to the deceased's belongings. They also coordinate the funeral processes.

Before the introduction by settlers and missionaries of Christian funeral practices, generational kin would have been responsible for burial. This typically occurred immediately after death. The body would be moved into nature, away from camp, in order to decay naturally until reburial.

The Ngarinyin community in North Kimberley built a rock mound around the body. The Yoingus in northeast Amhem Land placed the body in a hollowed painted log. With Western influence came the introduction of simple funerals, arranged by generational family members in consultation with elders and other relatives (Glaskin et al., 20).

The higher death rate among indigenous peoples and the frequency with which communities perform funerals might have suggested that practices surrounding death would become simpler. In fact, funeral customs are now more elaborate. Close mourners often wear outfits to distinguish themselves from others, such as a white top with black pants or a skirt. Funerals may be officiated by a Christian pastor or other religious leader, but members of the native community still have clear functions to perform.

In Martu communities the brothers, brothers-in-law, and grandsons of the deceased dig the grave, while the sisters, sisters-in-law, and wives smooth the gravesite. At the funeral, stories are told to remember the deceased. This is important if the pastor is not a community member.

At both the funeral and burial, ancestral songs are significant. The same songs are never sung at different funerals; instead, songs are composed according to the deceased's clan and lineage. Ancestral songs are strung together throughout the ceremonies. The order may be prearranged in consultation with elders and may be determined by the deceased's clan. Another consideration is the direction in which the spirit should be "sung home," for example, from inland to sea. Like the fights that erupt around cause of death, there may be disputes over song order.

Burial location also is of concern to indigenous people because it is where the spirit will remain permanently. Spirits watch over the communities in which they are buried. Visiting the grave to seek advice is a common practice for survivors to stay connected to ancestors. Most native people are buried in their mother's or father's homeland. The importance of extended relative networks can complicate the location. Someone may be born in a certain community but spend their life in another. Preference is to be buried near a close relative who will tend to the grave, keeping it tidy and leaving flowers on occasion (Jacklin, 184).

If being buried in a parent's homeland is not possible, one should be buried facing that direction. The traditional practice is to bury the dead where most appropriate according to the deceased's community status. Higher-status locations are those near the site of common rituals or in the center of camp. With Western influence, however, came the increased use of Christian cemeteries, though some communities still follow the traditional indigenous burial customs.

Once the location is determined, the burial generally is considered more important than the funeral ceremony, since the latter was only adopted after Western influence. Older traditions dictated that the family members closest to the deceased did not attend the burial and instead waited for generational kin and other community members to return from the burial site. Martu communities still observe this custom.

In most parts of the country everyone attends the burial, at which key mourners may again make public expressions of grief such as wailing. Some may hold on to the coffin and lament, "Why did you leave me?" Others may threaten to throw themselves into the grave. Regardless of the reality of the threat, this demonstrates extreme sadness for the loss. A smoking ceremony may be performed in which a fire is built near the grave. Attendees waft the smoke toward others. The ceremony is meant to encourage the spirit to accept its death and join the ancestral line.

The burial was traditionally only temporary until the bones were exhumed for the final ceremony. The time between these events was when key mourners would identify themselves with the deceased by entering into semiseclusion. These mourners observe the restraints of not eating meat, not engaging in sexual relations, and not remarrying.

Other tasks, known as "finishing up," include burning or distributing the deceased's belongings and sweeping the entire settlement, especially where the person lived and visited frequently. These activities symbolize the deceased's removal from the community. They also acknowledge the deceased by tending to the material presence that was left behind.

Reburial Ceremony

The final ceremony in the indigenous mourning process is reburial, performed anywhere from one to five years following death. Reburial remains a critical event, as it lifts restrictions placed on close mourners. A traditional reburial ceremony involves exhuming and cleaning the bones by generational relatives to prepare the spirit for its final burial. Fat and red ochre are applied to the bones, representing life and blood. The bones are wrapped in bark or leaves, symbolizing the mother's womb.

Reburial connects the deceased to the cycle of life and prepares the spirit for its final entrance into the ancestral world. The wrapped bones are presented to key mourners, who decide where to place them in the deceased's ancestral country. The bones often are placed in a cave associated with paternal ties. This combined with the mother's representational womb serves as an appropriate resting place to connect the deceased to her or his ancestry.

In most communities the reburial is no longer performed literally, particularly due to Western discomfort with the process. Instead, this type of reburial custom serves as a final remembrance of the departed loved one and another chance for family members to reconnect.

The ceremony is not performed on a specific date and instead is scheduled according to the availability of close relatives. It may be coordinated with other occasions such as a youth initiation or another funeral. Whenever it occurs, significant burial practices remain. Close mourners gather with extended family and those who knew the deceased. All able men from the deceased's family hunt for plains kangaroo to present to the mourners who have been refraining from eating meat. Because of their reluctance to break the taboo, the hunters rub the meat on the mourners' lips to indicate it is acceptable to eat meat again. The meat also is symbolic of the deceased.

Thus, eating it is considered a reincorporation of the deceased into the family's life. The family members may end their mourning, but the deceased will be with them in spirit forever.

Other gifts are given to the family as the mourning period ends. Blankets are especially comforting and womb-like. They remind the family of the real reburial process that would traditionally take place at this time. Because bones are no longer exhumed, some communities use the reburial ceremony to remember the deceased in other ways, such as unveiling a tombstone. This practice serves as a final goodbye and public acknowledgment of the deceased. Gifts are placed around the grave to be randomly distributed to family members.

Tombstones used to list only the deceased's name and birth and death dates. These markers have become more elaborate since the mid-nineteenth century. Markers now may include up to 400 words about the person's work and volunteer activities. Clan or family identification often appears as well.

The reburial ceremony signals that the spirit is not as dangerous as was previously perceived. It now is officially part of the ancestral world.

Ongoing Support for Mourners

Despite the final ceremony, relationships with the deceased's spirit and ancestors continue throughout a mourner's life. Spirits generally are not seen except by the very old and very young and are felt as a presence. The spirit lives near its grave along with others buried nearby and becomes part of the ancestral world, watching over the community and providing guidance and support.

The Coen people in central Cape York Peninsula have near daily interactions with spirits. The spirits may portend a positive or negative event, provide a source of historical knowledge about the family or community, or offer encouragement in the face of difficulties, such as land disputes with the Australian government.

The indigenous regularly visit graves of the deceased, believing that the spirit can serve as an intermediary with God when they are facing trying times. The spirit represents a connection to the past, present, and future. Among Australians, understanding the importance of death to indigenous communities is an ongoing study. National Sorry Day is recognized annually on May 26 to remember indigenous Australians who have died, particularly in wars with settlers or serving in the Australian military. Unfortunately, the day is not widely acknowledged.

In 1966 the Australian government recognized native culture by featuring a prominent artist's work on a one-dollar bill. A point mostly missed was that the currency featured a common indigenous funeral practice. This indicates the importance of death and funerals in indigenous life and the desire for recognition by Australian citizens (Attwood, 184).

Some indigenous elders believe that funerals are becoming too elaborate and that communities should return to simpler traditions observed before Western influence. This would reassert individuality and autonomy. Regardless of adjustments made to funeral ceremonies, the rituals and their meanings will remain significant to indigenous culture. Because opportunities to come together are infrequent, funerals allow communities to not only mourn a death but also perform other business. Another's reburial, acknowledgment of marriages, and settling disputes are all activities that might coincide with a funeral.

Ultimately, a death is a chance to reaffirm the community's strength. The speed and sincerity with which the indigenous respond to a death ensure that the family will be supported and that no one will grieve alone. Taken together, indigenous mourning rituals acknowledge the strength of younger generations and the significance of family ties. The customs also recognize the ancestors' role in maintaining attachments to the past and supporting communities into the future.

CHAPTER 20

Death and Mourning
in Japan

Japan, the world's 11th most populous country, has a unique history and a rich, singular culture. Populated as early as 30,000 BCE by a combination of native peoples and settlers from the Asian mainland, Japan first appeared in written texts from China in the first century.

While China would have a large influence on the island nation's early history, geographic and political isolationism allowed Japan to develop a culture distinct from the mainland. This includes the nation's rituals related to death and mourning, which are unlike any in the world.

Two religions historically have held the most sway on Japan's culture. Shinto is an animist religion that grew from folk tales of spirits and essences and is considered Japan's traditional religion. Buddhism, introduced from Korea and China, gradually developed unique Japanese sects (Nakata, n.p.).

While different rulers throughout the country's history promoted one religion over the other, eventually Shinto and Buddhist traditions commingled. Today, while most Japanese identify as nonsecular, life events often include aspects of both Shinto and Buddhism, including common practices for mourning a loved one.

Cultural Perspective on Death

Shinto and Buddhism have opposing views on death and mourning. This dichotomy informs the Japanese cultural perspective on death (Perez, n.p.). In the Shinto religion the world is inhabited by *kami*, or god-spirits, that are worshipped at shrines. Maintaining the purity of these shrines and their inhabiting god-spirits is of utmost importance.

When a person dies, he or she become a spirit. This spirit is akin to a ghost, with the potential to negatively affect the purity of shrines near the location of death. Specific rituals must be performed to protect the *kami* and appease the spirit of the dead, guiding it to the spirit world. In contrast, Japanese Buddhism views death as a natural, favorable transition of the soul between planes of existence. The practices surrounding death aim to offer comfort to the survivors (Bolitho, 17).

Nearly all funerals in Japan adhere to the broad structure and traditions of Buddhist customs, including a wake, a funeral, and a cremation ceremony. Many of the specific rituals, however, are Shinto in origin. The Shinto worldview influences many aspects of the funeral (Wiren, n.p.).

One significant distinction between Japanese and Western culture is their differing opinions on suicide. Historically, Japanese society has valued honor over life. Suicide has been used to regain lost honor (Pulvers, n.p.). In feudal Japan, it was expected for a samurai commander to commit ritual suicide, or *seppuku*, if his army was defeated in battle. More recent incidents were seen during World War II when Japanese kamikaze pilots intentionally crashed their aircraft into American ships and planes.

Today, most suicides are committed by high school students who have failed college entrance exams, middle-aged men who cannot find work, and elderly widows. The connection between suicide and honor has largely disappeared. Most Japanese have a neutral to negative attitude toward taking one's life.

At the Time of Death

Traditionally, the deceased's eldest son is responsible for making arrangements after death, although often a spouse or other relative will serve as "chief mourner" due to an eldest son's absence or out of respect for the wishes of the departed.

In death's immediate aftermath, the deceased's lips are moistened with *matsugo-no-mizu*, "water of the last moment." The body will be cleaned, and the orifices will then be stuffed with cotton. The deceased will be packed with dry ice and covered with a white sheet. Today this process typically is done at the hospital. The custom had been that preparing the body was done by the family at home, allowing the deceased to spend a final night in her or his own bed surrounded by loved ones and the special possessions enjoyed during life.

Makura-kazari, a small table with offerings of flowers, incense, and foods, is next to the bed. The family decorates a *butsudan*, a Buddhist prayer altar. The altar also commemorates other deceased relatives. Should the home also have a Shinto shrine, or *kamidana*, it will be wrapped in protective white paper. This reflects the Shinto belief that death is impure.

The Wake, Funeral, and Cremation Ceremonies

The first of the traditional ceremonies is the wake. The wake may occur the night immediately following death. However, in most cases the event will be postponed a few days to allow travel time for family and friends. The wake, customarily, is the event attended by the most people, with the funeral reserved for immediate family and very close friends.

Prior to the wake, the body will be cleaned and face makeup applied to give the deceased a more lifelike look. Traditionally, the body then would be dressed in a white kimono. In recent times, many men have been dressed in a suit instead. If a kimono is chosen, it will be wrapped with the right side over the left. In life, it is culturally unacceptable to wrap a kimono this way due to its connotation with death.

At the wake, attendees bring gifts of cash to give to the chief mourner. The amount is determined by each attendee's relationship to the deceased. A comparatively distant acquaintance may give only 30 dollars. Attendees closer to the deceased may give thousands of dollars. Wealthy attendees give even more. This money is used to pay funeral expenses, tip workers, and purchase commemorative gifts for those in attendance.

Wakes traditionally are held in Buddhist temples. Many Japanese families have begun holding wakes in their homes or in public spaces due to the cost of reserving a temple. Wherever it is held, a Buddhist priest generally leads the wake, chanting Buddhist scripture, or sutras, to honor the dead and comfort the living. The deceased's coffin will sit at the back of the temple or site of the wake. Attendees take turns coming forward to offer respects and light ceremonial incense. After all attendees have had a turn, the wake ends. The closest family and friends will spend the night celebrating the life of their departed loved one over food and drinks, a custom called *okiyome*. It is entirely acceptable for guests to drink to excess during *okiyome*.

The following day, close relatives and friends will gather for the funeral. This ceremony is more formal than the wake. Attendees dress in black, suits for men and dresses or kimonos for women. As at the wake, the guests will burn incense, and the priest will offer sutras. The priest will give the deceased a new Buddhist name, or *kaimyo*. Longer *kaimyos* are more auspicious and are often reserved for those whose family has made a large donation to the Buddhist temple.

After the funeral, the coffin is loaded into a decorated hearse and taken to the cremation facility. Prior to World War II, bodies typically were buried. Buddhist-affiliated sites were considered preferable. Today, most Japanese are cremated due to lack of land for burial and the purity associated with fire. Even members of Japan's imperial family have requested cremation rather than internment in elaborate tombs (Greenwood, n.p.).

While cremation in the United States often is performed behind the scenes, in Japan it is an essential part of the mourning process. It is attended by the same friends and family as the funeral. The guests assist in loading the coffin into the cremator. The chief mourner presses the button igniting the flame. Attendees wait until cremation is complete. The family then engages in *kotsuage*, a bone-picking ceremony. They sift through the ashes with special chopsticks hunting bones of good fortune. Head bones are associated with intelligence. The most important bone is a neck bone, the hyoid, resembling Buddha in prayer. Relatives use chopsticks to pass bones to each other, depositing them in an urn. This is the only time it is acceptable to share things with chopsticks (Perez, n.p.).

Mourning and Remembrance

After the ceremonies the mourning period begins. During the medieval Edo period, the imperial class was aligned with the Shinto religion. Japanese rulers set strict standards for how long individuals should be mourned and how long their loved ones should abstain from work and other activities. Time periods varied according to the importance of the deceased and how close an individual was to her or him. "Mourning edicts" changed as rulers changed (Hirai, 44).

The longest mourning periods were reserved for heads of households, public officials, and members of the ruling class. Mourning might last for months or even years. As Buddhism replaced Shinto as the rulers' official religion, Japan's mourning rituals and time frame gave way to a more standardized set of practices. These customs are observed in Japan today.

Following the wake, the funeral, and the cremation, the urn with bones and ashes is kept at home. Another ceremony is held every seven days, reflecting Buddhism's seven factors of enlightenment. After 49 days, the bones and ashes are either scattered or interred in a grave of some kind (Perez, n.p.).

Gravesites often are adorned with a simple marker. Sometimes a small basket is at the gravesite. In this receptacle a visitor may leave a business card to notify the deceased's family that a visit has been made. Sites associated with Buddhism are the most preferable locations for graves. One such site is the final resting place of Kobo Daishi, the founder of Buddhism's Shingon sect. The graveyard surrounding his mausoleum atop Mount Koya has more than 200,000 tombstones. Many families opt to scatter loved one's ashes there without a formal grave.

Due to the cost of land in Japan, many wishing to have a marker honoring their loved one have turned to the relatively new phenomenon of "grave apartments." Often located in high-rise apartment buildings housing Buddhist temples, these digital mausoleums have alcoves for cremated remains and a screen displaying photographs of the deceased (Martin, n.p.). Relatives and friends can stop by to honor those who have died. This twenty-first-century accommodation reflects Japan's nimble nature to modernize while still holding on to tradition (Becker, 90).

The most significant event associated with mourning in Japan is the annual Obon festival (Perez, n.p.). Obon takes place over three days. It is commonly observed in August, with certain regions marking the occasion in July, or the seventh month of the lunar calendar. Obon is like the Day of the Dead celebrated in Mexico. Workers are granted leave to reunite with their families and honor the departed. Households hang lanterns outside their doors to attract the spirits. Mourners offer gifts at gravesites and Buddhist temples. Obon culminates with the *bon odori*, a folk dance attracting and celebrating spirits of the dead. The dance differs from region to region, reflecting each area's history and character. The most famous *bon odori* festival takes place in Kyoto, where five enormous bonfires shaped like Japanese characters are set ablaze on the surrounding mountains.

CHAPTER 21

Chinese Views of Death

To comprehend Chinese attitudes toward death, it is necessary to understand the country's cultural history. Confucianism, Taoism, and Buddhism have been the most influential religions on Chinese thought. These philosophies are the foundation for perspectives on life and death. Confucianism, named for its founder, was the country's most influential religion. Taoism was created by Lao Zi around the sixth century BCE. Lao Zi's masterpiece "The Classic of the Virtue of the Tao" establishes the religion's basic principles. Buddhism was introduced to China from India between 58 and 76 CE and began to flourish in the third century.

Chinese society does not have a strong inclination toward religion. Yet, these three traditional philosophies are highly influential in everyday life. Each of these belief systems has its own understanding of death.

Confucianism

Confucianism is concerned with morality and the ordering of social conduct. It is not considered a religion so much as an ethical system. In Confucianism, the hereafter, paradise, and hell do not exist. Confucianism, focuses on the here and now, leaving the afterlife as an afterthought. Confucianism does accept the existence of a soul in the hereafter. It is not, however, something over which people obsess. For Confucius, examining death is a worthwhile study for which there are no definitive answers. The philosophy teaches that the essence of life and death is assuming responsibility for the welfare of others.

Confucianism prioritizes life over death. Confucius questioned how one could know about death before comprehending life (Wei-Ming, 35). The philosophy rejects reincarnation and does not accept the idea of new life after death.

Confucianism's teachings emphasize the moral obligation of individuals to strive for self-improvement. The collective aim is the creation of an ideal harmonious society. The cultivation of an individual's virtues is the heart of the philosophy. The ultimate goal is to harmonize behavior so that humanity becomes one with the cosmos. Confucianism squarely focuses on individual responsibility during one's lifetime. Its teachings relegate the afterlife to a secondary consideration. Immortality only takes on ethical significance in the spirit realm and is not linked with daily life (Wei-Ming and Tucker, 2).

Confucius downplayed death. Life should be devoted to becoming a sage for the betterment of humankind. Confucianism does not have special rituals for death. Its ceremonies are like Buddhist customs.

Buddhism

An observant Buddhist may achieve transcendence from death. The transition beyond this life is a gate through which consciousness passes. A well-practiced Buddhist journeys to a new life. Death terminates the body. The spirit lives on, attaching to a new body to launch a new life.

Students of Buddhism understand the power of meditation. Each meditation session is a rehearsal for the moment of death. Devoted practitioners transcend several states of consciousness on their way to enlightenment. The states are classified as sravakas, pratyeka-buddhas, bodhisattvas, and buddhas (Khadro, 19).

People who cause suffering for others must transmigrate through various stages of suffering. These realms are heavens, auras, humans, animals, hungry ghosts, and hells. A new life is the sum of one's experiences and the actions taken as a result of those experiences. The accumulated wisdom is karma.

Buddhist Rituals

Buddhist mourning observances extend 49 days. The first seven are the most intense. Prayers are recited every seven days for seven weeks. If the deceased's family is poor, ceremonies may be for just three days. At the 49-day mark the family stops bringing rice to their home altar. The next milestone is 100 days following death, when mourners observe the "end of the tears." Mourning ends on the death's second anniversary.

During the seven-week period, family and friends convene at the deceased's home to share a meal and remembrances. The food generally is a vegan spread consisting of fermented tofu and steamed vegetables. Although the food may get monotonous, it sustains the mourners. In Buddhist culture, the family's perseverance during mourning is a show of support for the deceased, providing a solid send-off to the afterlife.

Chinese Buddhists chant "Amitabha" to help the dying person remain peaceful. Buddhist belief holds that people are aware throughout the dying process and can sense their spirit leaving their body. During the separation, atmosphere is important. Consciousness would experience pain if the environment is disrupted or the body is moved. Thus, the deceased is left still for eight hours.

Death rituals are guided by two principles: purification of bad karmas and accumulation of merits. Activities related to death are classified into rituals of elevation and acts of merits. Elevation customs consist of chanting accompanied by musical instruments and sutras. With flowers, incense, and various foods, the holy buddha will prostrate for the deceased. Prayers of repentance on behalf of the departed are recited. Donations to religious and other charities are offered as expressions of merit and moral standards.

Artificial currency is burned during funeral rituals. Bills are made of paper and adorned with gold or silver foil. Each has auspicious signs and words printed on the foil. Currency includes images of deities known as hell bank notes. These bills are offerings to heavenly and earthly deities.

For contemporary Chinese, Buddhist customs provide guidance

for conducting oneself in the aftermath of a loved one's death. This adherence holds even if the rituals are not fully understood. The belief is that the spirit of the ancestors splits time between the grave and the afterworld. The afterworld is not thought to be heaven or hell. Rather, existence in the afterlife resembles one's time on Earth.

Taoism

The goal in Taoism is to achieve tao, meaning to find the way. In Taoism, birth is not a beginning, and death is not an end. Death is not to be feared or desired. Instead, priority is given to enjoying life. The afterlife is downplayed. Eternal life is achieved on Earth. Death is not the endpoint. It is the crossroads where one's essence can be found.

The longer one lives, the closer to tao one comes. The hope is to become immortal, to achieve tao, to reach a deeper life. The afterlife is to be in harmony with the universe. Instead of losing life upon death, Taoism teaches that death is a transformation. The deceased participates in an endless, ever-changing dance of manifestation, existence, and de-manifestation. That is the way of tao (Wong, 190).

Mortal existence is simply one of the infinite manifestations of tao. The philosophy advises elimination of the instinctive thought that death is bad. Taoism's adherents should not view death as a negative "ultimate end." Its followers should rest comfortably knowing that what happens after mortal death is part of the eternal process of tao.

Taoist Customs

Taoist rituals for the dead are performed with the understanding that death is a continuation of life into a new phase. The customs are intended to guide the wandering soul to its new home. Descendants offer prayers and acts of penance on the deceased's behalf. Survivors believe that their ancestor's soul always is watching over them.

The ceremony conducted for the deceased is called "preparing the path for the dead." A home altar is adorned with pictures of 11 gods. Tea, rice, and water are put in cups in front of the altar. Tea symbolizes yin, water is the energy of yang, and rice represents the union of the two. A Taoist priest explains to the gods of the afterworld the deceased's good deeds. The priest seeks forgiveness for the wrongdoings of the departed. Cymbals are struck to accompany the priest's prayer for safe passage to the afterworld.

An incense bowl representing refinement and purification is kept burning for 49 days and nights following the funeral. The burning incense symbolizes the soul, known as the inner energies. The name and dates of birth and death are inscribed on special paper.

Funeral Rituals

Because the Chinese do not follow any specific tradition, they seldom adhere to a single religion's customs. Most prefer a hybrid approach. Proper burial is of great concern. Cremation is rare. Improper funeral arrangements can damage a family's fortune and wreak disaster. Funeral and burial rites are determined largely by the age of the deceased, the manner of death, the departed's position in society, and marital status.

Before death, preparation for a funeral begins. When one is close to dying, a coffin will be ordered by the family. When it is time to nail the coffin shut, yellow holy papers are pasted to it. These are meant to rid the evil spirits that disturb the peace of the deceased. Those present avoid watching this part of the ceremony, as watching is considered bad luck.

Pallbearers remove the coffin from the house, with the head facing the road. More holy papers and prayers are pasted on the coffin. The casket is placed in a hearse that proceeds slowly. The eldest family members follow the oldest child, whose forehead is bowed against the hearse.

According to the guidance of feng shui, Chinese burials usually occur on hillsides. One belief holds that the higher on the hillside one is buried, the better served he will be. Mourners wear any color except red. The belief is that the deceased will become a ghost if red is worn. Prayers are recited by the cemetery keeper after the coffin is covered. As a token of gratitude, the deceased's family gives a small red packet with money to those present.

The traditional belief is that the corpse represents powers extending beyond death. These powers can affect the fate of the living. Mourners might ask an expert to analyze feng shui to determine the time, location, and orientation of the body. Chinese officials have condemned this practice and set limits to prevent it from becoming mainstream. They consider such observance superstitious.

After Death

The furniture and artwork in the deceased's home are covered with red cloth. All mirrors in the home are removed to avoid seeing reflections of the deceased's coffin or ghost. It is believed that once the mirror reflects the coffin, another member of the mourner's family might soon die. A white cloth is hung in the doorway of the home. A gong is placed outside the front door. If a male has died, the gong is set on the left side of the doorway. If a female has died, it is placed on the right side.

During the wake, an altar with white candles and incense is placed at the feet of the corpse. Special paper and prayer money is burned throughout the wake to ensure that the deceased has plenty of currency in the afterlife. Friends and neighbors light incense and bow to the deceased. To help defray funeral expenses, attendees may deposit money in a donation box.

It is customary for male and female relatives and women outside the family to wail at wakes to express sorrow. Those who sob receive the blessings of the deceased. The volume of the wailing corresponds to the extent of the inheritance. The larger the fortune, the louder the cries.

Card playing and other diversions may take place in the courtyard to distract family members from the details of the funeral. This is not considered disrespectful.

The mortal human is believed to consist of three *huns* (spirits) and seven *pos* (energies). When a person dies, one of these *huns* stays at the site of death. The second one remains within the deceased's body. The third *hun* is off to hell. All seven *pos* stay with the corpse.

According to Chinese tradition, on the seventh day following death the *hun* in hell returns to Earth to take the other two for judgment back in hell. The seventh day is the last time the deceased can come back as a ghost to see her or his family. This also is the first day *po* departs the body. After the seventh day, the deceased can never revive or reappear. The body can be buried. By the 49th day, all seven *pos* will have left the body. The deceased is said to have left the mortal world completely. The ghost will have been judged in hell. The ghost either would be left there to suffer as atonement for her or his sins or would be sent back to the mortal world for reincarnation.

A Festival to Honor the Dead

The Chinese observe an annual festival called Ching Ming. Held in early April, the celebration coincides with nature's seasonal rebirth. The event is similar to Mexico's Day of the Dead. People visit the gravesites of ancestors. They honor their loved ones by cleaning tombs and headstones. Families bring food, wine, and flowers. Being in bloom, daisies are the decoration of choice.

Attending the Ching Ming festival indicates reverence for the deceased. Some families burn incense and artificial money in front of the grave, believing this to be the currency in the other world. Legend has it that if the observance is not performed well the family will be deemed disrespectful. The upset soul will bring misfortune to the family.

Comforting Actions

Chinese mourning practices are a mix of traditional folklore, superstition, and philosophical belief systems. Because there is no single predominant religion in contemporary China, Confucianism,

Taoism, and Buddhism mingle to influence the country's attitudes toward life and death.

In China, devotion of sons and daughters reflects sincere ancestral reverence. Attempting to grant one's final wish is considered a way to honor the deceased. The effort itself can be a comfort to mourners.

Returning to Buddhism as Self-Salvation

Many Chinese turn to Buddhism when they are facing the confusion and desperation of the end of their own life. Some believe that the philosophy addresses the fear that accompanies death. Buddhism speaks to an afterlife as part of the cycle of existence. One learns to confront suffering by practicing Buddhist customs. Buddhism provides a peaceful bridge to the afterlife. Each meditation session is a rehearsal for one's transition to the next destination of her or his life's journey.

Chinese celebrities have embraced Buddhism, despite public skepticism that the belief is no more than superstition. Among the famous who have adopted the philosophy are singers Li Na and Faye Wong and kung fu stars Jet Li and Zhao Wenzhou. After being diagnosed with cancer, actress turned successful businesswoman Chen Xiaoxu shocked Chinese society in 2007 with her conversion to Buddhism.

One of the greatest acts of kindness for a Buddhist is helping another accept death peacefully and positively. Buddhism recognizes the strong emotional and spiritual needs of the dying. These needs must be protected, respected, and guided when one experiences suffering. Many Chinese turn to Buddhism in their dying days, believing that it will bring peace and comfort to their souls. These individuals adhere to Buddhist practices to seek salvation, tranquility, and enlightenment.

CHAPTER 22

Islamic Mourning Rituals

Founded in the seventh century by the prophet Muhammad, Islam has grown to become one of the world's largest religions, with more than one billion followers. Muslims adhere to five pillars of faith:

1. Salaat, the prayer offered five times a day;
2. Zakat, giving alms;
3. Ramadan, the annual period of fasting;
4. Hajj, the pilgrimage to the holy land Mecca; and
5. Shahadah, the declaration of faith that there is no god but Allah and that Muhammad is the prophet of God [Islamic Relief UK].

The fifth tenet is most significant because those principles are the foundation upon which Muslim life is based. Most Islamic beliefs are found in the Quran, the holy book containing the Word of God. Muslims also model their behavior on the sunna and hadiths, the living example and sayings of the Prophet Muhammad.

Sharia, or Islamic law, is derived from these sources and instructs Muslims on how to live. Although there is no official religious hierarchy in Islam, respected leaders and scholars have written widely accepted works that interpret the Quran and Muhammad's teachings.

The most notable book relating experiences of death is al-Durra (The Precious Pearl), which describes what becomes of the soul. As Muslims draw from a few specific texts and sources of knowledge, there is relative uniformity in Muslim life, including how followers understand death, practices surrounding it, and expectations for those in mourning. There are some variations in the interpretation of customs based on traditions in effect before the rise of the religion and depending on local practices. But there are certain actions undertaken by all observant Muslims mourning the loss of a loved one.

Death is considered by Muslims to be the fulfillment of life's work. The deeds of an individual during her or his lifetime impact how the individual is judged in death. Muslims do good deeds in this world, bearing in mind the hereafter.

When Muslims die, they visit heaven to receive an initial judgment. They are then transported back to the grave to await the Day of Resurrection, when everyone on Earth perishes and the dead rise from their graves. On the Day of Judgment, God reads an individual's book of deeds and uses the scales of justice to determine whether the person lived a good life. Those sent to heaven will live in God's presence forever, along with prophets and martyrs who are positioned closest to God. Nonbelievers and those hypocritical in their faith are banished to eternal hellfire. Some Muslims may spend time in hell for their sins before entering heaven.

While Muslims strive to do good in the world, Islam also teaches that no one is perfect. God shows mercy to those who have made sincere effort to live according to His teachings. God's mercy and power to control life also extend to death.

Muslims believe that God chooses when each person dies. One should not question God's decision but should accept death as a fact of life. Because Muslims were created from God, death is simply life's next stage. The individual returns to be with God. Muslims may be comforted by the fact their loved one will live in the hereafter in God's presence.

Since the religion was formed centuries ago, Islamic leaders have discouraged excessive funeral practices, calling instead for simple, swift burial preparations. Uniformity is emphasized so that most practices of a Muslim funeral appear similar all over the world (Ross, 83).

While the customs may seem simplistic, when combined with the emphasis on accepting God's will these rituals serve as a source of comfort. The process encourages mourners to minimize their fear and despair when confronting death.

At the Time of Death

Because murder, suicide, and euthanasia are forbidden in Islam, deaths should occur naturally, with time for family and friends to gather around their loved one. It is preferable to die at home to ensure that relatives are present, but they also may gather at the hospital if necessary. Muslims strive to prepare for death by giving and seeking forgiveness and settling debts. This also is a time for saying goodbyes.

The dying individual should lie or, if possible, sit facing Mecca. This eases the soul's eventual journey. As death nears, family and friends encourage the dying person to repent for his sins and turn his thoughts toward God. Muslims strive to make their last words the shahadah, the declaration of faith. If the dying person is too weak, his family will whisper it in his ear (Webb, 111). This declaration is especially poignant, as it is also whispered when a baby is born. So, it is announced at the beginning and end of life. This is consistent with accounts of nurse midwifes who also serve as death doulas. They say that the sensation in the room is similar when a soul enters the world as when one leaves.

Friends and family offer hope to the dying individual about God's mercy. They may recite passages from the Quran to comfort the dying and her loved ones and ensure that the end of life is filled with faith and hope for whatever comes. After death, the deceased's eyes and mouth are closed. His arms are laid at his sides, and he is covered by a clean sheet.

Reaction to Death

One of the greatest discrepancies among Muslim communities is the reaction to death. Because death is seen as God's will, loved ones should not question this fate and should react with patience and resignation. While grief is expected and weeping is acceptable, Muslims emphasize calm in the face of death. Displays of sorrow should not be excessive.

Before the rise of Islam, women were regarded for the poetry of their laments and the beauty of the dirges they sang. For women, common reactions to death include crying, wailing, breast beating, tearing at hair, scratching the face, and the ripping of clothes. Vivid reactions were outward expressions of inner grief. Sometimes professional mourners were paid to sing and wail along with the deceased's female family members (Halevi, 3).

Although the Quran is silent on wailing, during the formation and initial practices of Islam, leaders and scholars widely interpreted excessive reactions to death to be uncivilized. Worse still, crying out against death was seen as a form of questioning God's will, which is forbidden and may prevent the soul from advancing on its spiritual journey.

The tension between the women's strong reaction and the desire to be calm in the face of death exists to this day. Some communities insist that reactions to death be muted, while others tolerate more excessive shows of grief. Many communities also forbade women from attending funerals to ensure they did not openly lament death, a restriction that persists.

Muslim female and male behaviors in the aftermath of death represent two of the most common reactions: intense grief and quiet acceptance. Regardless of individual response, relatives pray for the deceased to be forgiven and begin funeral arrangements immediately.

Preparation for Burial

Because Muslims believe in swift judgment of the soul, the deceased should be buried before sundown on the day of death or within 24 hours if delay is necessary. There is no embalming, makeup, or finery for the deceased, nor is there a wake, an extended eulogy, or a fancy coffin. There is a simple ritual washing, a shrouding in plain white cloth (kafan), and a funeral prayer about five minutes long. The burial follows. The body preferably is placed directly into the earth. When required by law, the body may be buried in a basic coffin (Jonker, 47).

A relative or community leader may announce the death and the time and place of burial. This informs the community when prayers will be offered for the deceased. This notice also signals to relatives and friends when to attend the funeral and show support for the family.

Upon one's last breath, he or she is visited by the Angel of Death. This is when the soul initially is removed. The extraction is gentle for those who have performed good deeds and lived faithfully and are thus headed for heaven. The soul's emergence is more difficult for those lacking in good deeds and headed in a less heavenly direction.

A worthy soul is shepherded to heaven, where it may view the vision of God and receive initial judgment. It is then returned to the body to await the Day of Resurrection. Because the soul remains in the body, cremation and embalming are forbidden. Autopsies are discouraged unless necessary. Organ donation, once forbidden, has been accepted in some communities as a good deed to save another's life.

Ritual washing of the body is performed within hours of a Muslim's death, usually by a family member of the same gender or by a professional or trusted person in the community. Sometimes a wife may wash her husband. People of either sex can wash a young child. It is an honor and a good deed to wash the deceased before burial. To give a body its final cleansing comes with immense reward: the erasure of 40 major sins from one's lifetime record. Because the final cleaning is such a detailed ritual, mosques have volunteers ready to assist grieving families. Since the preference is to die at home, washing generally is performed there. It also may be done in a private room in the hospital or morgue. Like washing oneself prior to prayers, washing the body prepares the deceased for the ceremony and burial to await final judgment.

The body is treated with great care and attended to at all times before burial. The body is never exposed. In the ritual Islamic bathing, the body is given utmost respect. The deceased stays covered. The washers are forever silent about any bodily irregularities observed. A scar, tattoo, or deformity is never mentioned. In the deceased's most vulnerable moments, he or she is guaranteed protection by family and community. The washing ritual is performed quietly and gently, as the spirit remains in the body. An imam, the community's religious leader, or a close relative may quietly recite passages from the Quran during the washing.

Body-washers wear sterile scrubs to protect them from whatever disease may have stricken the deceased. They tie on large paper aprons and pull on rubber gloves. Puffy paper sleeves that attach from elbow to wrist are tucked into the gloves. Big paper booties are worn. A face mask with a large transparent plastic eye shield is pulled into place.

Islamic tradition prescribes that comfortably warm water is used to bath the body. The deceased is washed three times with clean water and soap from head to toe, always starting with the right side. This side is favored by Muslims because the left is considered unclean. The order in which body parts are washed varies by community but generally includes the mouth, nose, head, hands, arms, and feet. A full body washing follows. Before the final cleansing, perfume may be added to the water to prepare the deceased for meeting with God.

Once the washing is complete, the deceased is shrouded in a clean plain cloth. Muslims usually use a white cloth free of stitches and adornments that may prevent the soul from easily leaving the body. Three sheets are normally used for men and five for women. The shroud for the head is wrapped separately so it can be removed for a brief final viewing. The viewing takes place before the body is moved to the site of the prayer ceremony and burial. This experience usually draws the most intense reactions from family and community members.

If wailing is tolerated in the community, women will cry and shout, sometimes holding the body and refusing to let go. The men may try to restrain the women and encourage a calm reaction, looking stoically at the deceased for the last time. Tears may be silently shed.

Each person looking upon the deceased says a quiet prayer asking for mercy for their loved one and for themselves. Witnessing the deceased once more also serves as a reminder that death is part of life and that everyone should redouble their commitment to God and their effort to perform good deeds. After the final viewing, the shroud is replaced and the men carry the body to the funeral ceremony.

Prayer Ceremony

A short prayer ceremony is the final commemoration before burial. Prayers usually are recited at the mosque, but the brief service may be performed in any quiet place if necessary. This ceremony is considered the most important preparation prior to burial. Prayers said by the congregation ask God for forgiveness for the deceased's sins and seek God's mercy for the departed loved one in the hereafter. Usually this service is attended only by men. The worshippers line up in rows, with the body placed in front of the congregation. If women are present, they may watch quietly behind the men in the back of the room.

The ceremony is led by an imam, who may be a close male relative of the deceased. A trusted member of the community also may officiate. The leader stands at the head of the deceased. Most of the prayers are recited quietly to show respect to the departed. This tone helps ensure that the ceremony does not devolve into an excessive display of grief. The portions of the service that are spoken aloud are the greeting and the prayers in which the imam asks for mercy for the deceased and for all in attendance. The congregation quietly says individual prayers on the deceased's behalf. Talking is prohibited.

When the prayer ceremony ends, the imam stands in front of the congregation. The men form two lines behind him. They carry the body in a procession to the burial site. Six at a time, men shoulder the burden of moving the body. Each man declares the shahadah. It is a good deed to be part of the procession, a final favor that can never be returned.

Women generally do not join the procession or attend the burial. If they are permitted to do so, it is with the understanding that they will quietly follow the procession, will not make an excessive showing of grief, and will leave immediately after the burial.

Burial Ceremony

Even if a coffin was used to transport the body from washing to prayers to the funeral, the preference is to be buried in a simple shroud. This is intended to ease the body's return to the earth.

The grave is dug with a smaller, deeper chamber in the middle into which the body is lowered. A close male relative places the body in the chamber in a sleeplike position on its right side, with the head facing Mecca. Wooden boards are placed over the chamber, creating a small space for the body. Everyone present shovels earth into the grave.

The tone at the funeral is respectful. The imam recites passages from the Quran while individuals quietly pray for the deceased or declare the shahadah. Everyone remains standing until the grave is filled. Once this communal task is done, the men crouch around the grave, lifting their hands toward the heavens. The imam leads a final collective prayer.

Everyone exits the funeral quickly in silence. Close relatives may linger. The imam remains to recite a few final blessings for the deceased. Although the departed are no longer of this world, they may continue to earn blessings based on what they have left behind through righteous offspring who pray for their forgiveness, through knowledge they have spread to others, or through charitable work whose effects outlive them.

Muslims believe that shortly after burial, the soul is visited by two angels who question the deceased's beliefs. The imam may stay to counsel the departed on her or his answers. The questions vary by community but include the following:

Who is your God? (My God is Allah)
Who is your prophet? (My prophet is Muhammad)
Which is your book? (My book is the Quran)

If the soul answers properly, it will become comfortable in its space as it awaits the Day of Resurrection. If it does not, it will feel cramped and suffocated and will be tormented by the angels. The answers to these questions influence how the soul is treated on the Day of Judgment.

The Mourning Period

Islamic tradition teaches resigned acceptance of death as part of life. This is epitomized by the expression "To God we belong, and to God we return." Grieving nonetheless is expected of relatives. The community plays an important role supporting the family in its grief (Yasien-Esmael and Rubin, 495).

The official mourning period, known as ma'tam, is three days. During this time the family does not cook. It is a good deed for community members to visit, offer condolences, and bring food. This support is particularly important for women, who stay home during the prayer ceremony and funeral while men gather at the mosque.

The family may arrange for recitations of the Quran throughout the mourning period. In more traditional communities, the recitations take place in front of the deceased's home for everyone to hear. More commonly, the recitations take place inside as family members receive visitors. Visitors focus on remembering the deceased and refrain from mundane matters. In addition, visitors encourage the family to stay strong in their religious beliefs and keep faith that God will show mercy to their loved one. Visitors may tell mourners that God will reward those who accept death with peaceful resignation. In turn, mourners offer thanks, telling visitors that God will favor them for being comforting during such difficult days.

An imam or community leader may visit several times to support the family during the mourning period. It is expected that everyone in the community will visit the family. It is only acceptable to visit after the third day if someone has had to travel a great distance to pay respects.

Mourners mark the third day after death, the end of the official mourning period, with a small gathering. Special foods are offered in memory of the deceased. After three days, mourners are expected to come to terms with their grief and return to normal life. The family bathes, changes clothes, cleans house, and gives away the deceased's belongings.

When reentering public life, although the mourning period has ended, women continue to represent the family and their loss by wearing a specific color. In some communities women wear white. In others, they wear black or another subdued hue. Younger women may wear the color of mourning for three months. Older women wear the color up to a year.

Continuing Comfort for the Family

Islamic practice does not call for further days to remember the dead beyond the official mourning period. Some communities create customs to provide the bereaved with ongoing comfort. Some families honor the seventh or tenth day after death with a gathering like that of the third day (Suhail, Oyebode, and Ajmal, 22).

A recent custom in some communities is for women to gather on the first Thursday after the death to eat sweets and hold an uplifting celebration of their loved one's life. Many communities commemorate the 40th day after death with a small ceremony and the telling of Prophet Muhammad's birth.

Regardless of which days are marked by the family, the Quran states that female widows must wait four months and ten days to remarry. This interval ensures that the woman is not pregnant with her deceased husband's child. This waiting period means that the community accepts the widow's remarriage, which often is a financial necessity.

The final day commonly observed by families is the one-year anniversary of death. The family and friends may place a small stone on the grave. The gathering should not be elaborate. Large tombstones are discouraged. Graves traditionally are identified with simple markers at ground level. More excessive displays sometimes mark modern graves.

Cemeteries have two functions in Muslim life. They serve as reminders of the certainty of death and the need to maintain a strong belief in God's mercy. They need not be tended too closely, since they only represent the physical world. The spiritual realm is more significant.

Beyond the official mourning period and other days of remembrance, many Muslims continue to honor loved ones in daily life. Families may hang a portrait of the deceased in their house and maintain a few mementos to remember the departed. Some recite the Quran daily in the name of the deceased. Others strive to be more like their loved one by performing good deeds or being kind or charitable to others. It is customary for families to make donations in honor of the deceased or even undertake a meaningful charitable project. Some may name a child after the deceased as a way to remember their loved one.

Family members often see the deceased in their dreams and share those experiences with others. Those dreams can be comforting and are believed to indicate that the soul is living peacefully in the hereafter. Shared holidays also offer opportunities to commemorate the dead. The month of Ramadan and Eid al-Adha, the festival that marks the end of Ramadan, are such occasions.

The teaching of Islam offers followers powerful ways to understand and cope with death. Muslims believe strongly that each death is God's will. They strive to react to death with resignation and faith. Those in mourning are supported by community members who encourage them to have strength in the face of death and remind them that they will be rewarded for doing so. While death represents the end of life in this world, the soul continues its spiritual journey.

Muslims believe in a merciful God. Those who have suffered the loss of a loved one can find comfort in knowing that God will show mercy in the hereafter to those who did good deeds and lived faithfully in this life.

CHAPTER 23

Hindu Mourning Rituals

Hinduism is a religion rich in history, drawing from diverse traditions to offer its nearly one billion followers worldwide a source of comfort during mourning. The Hindu religion teaches that when someone dies, the soul passes into another body. The belief in reincarnation is the foundation for Hindu funeral traditions. In accordance with reincarnation, Hindus sometimes describe death as changing clothes (Editors of *Hinduism Today* Magazine, 64).

Those who perform good deeds or actions (karma) and follow the natural laws (dharma) that guide behavior are promised that their soul (atman) will be reborn into a better life. The soul is liberated (moksa) from the cycle of rebirth (samsara) when it reaches full spiritual attainment. It is then absorbed into Brahman, the great spirit. For Hindus in mourning, the thought of rebirth or liberation can be comforting.

The beliefs reflect traditional Hindu practices, most of which occur in India, where Hinduism is the dominant religion. Mourning customs vary depending on where the family is from, where they live now, their socioeconomic status, and the religious sect to which they belong.

Elders and pandits (priests or scholarly experts) often are sought for guidance on how to observe funeral rituals, particularly if circumstances differ from traditional settings. When performing rituals, Hindus draw from several spiritual texts including the Vedas, the Upanishads, the Garuda Purana, and the Bhagavad Gita (Gupta, 244).

Preparing for Death

Hindus distinguish between a good and bad death. A bad death is one in which the deceased was unable to properly prepare for dying. Examples include deaths that are sudden, premature, or out of one's control. A good death is one in which the individual can prepare by addressing both physical and spiritual ties to the world. He or she can settle earthly issues such as finances and the distribution of possessions.

The dying individual can improve karmas to prepare for the afterlife by resolving disputes, saying goodbyes, doing penance for misdeeds, or making charitable offerings. Family and friends support such efforts by acknowledging the dying persons' requests and accommodating their retreat from obligations as they enter the final stage of life.

After making necessary preparations, the dying person surrounds one's self with loved ones and ensures that proper rituals will be performed before, at, and after death. This enables the spirit to more easily depart the body and enter the afterlife. As a conscious death is ideal to keep the mind focused, Hindus may refrain from numbing medicines close to death (Brahmaprana, 337).

When death is imminent, relatives keep constant vigil. Family, friends, and community members may begin paying their respects at this time. Sometimes a close female family member, usually the wife, will refuse to believe that the person is dying. She will fast, pray, sing hymns (bhajans), and recite holy texts in the hope of restoring health. Spiritual advisers may visit to support these efforts. Others, realizing that death is imminent, may only talk about the situation in vague terms.

The ideal death occurs on the banks of the sacred Ganges River. Most Hindus, however, die at home. The dying person is placed on the floor or ground because it puts her or him closer to Mother Earth, the source of all life. This placement allows the spirit to exit the body more easily. The top of the person's head usually is pointed north, known as the direction of mankind. The face is pointed south, the direction of Yama, the god of death. This positioning facilitates the spirit's bodily departure, making it easier for Yama to transport the spirit into the afterlife.

At the Time of Death

Close relatives stay by the dying person's side even if he does not request it. They help him pray, chant his mantra, and focus his thoughts on God. Dying alone is not preferred. Hindus believe that the dying individual would be too worried about his family to concentrate on God. Thinking holy thoughts at the time of death improves one's karma and impacts the soul's fate after death. If someone is unconscious as he is dying, a family member may whisper to him his mantra or God's name.

Immediately before death, Ganges water and a leaf or two of tulsi (a sacred Hindu plant) are placed in the mouth to satisfy thirst and hunger. At the time of death, female relatives may wail in emotional outbursts. If death is unexpected or its exact time is unknown, the Ganges water and tulsi can be placed in the mouth as soon as possible thereafter. A coin is placed in each hand as payment for crossing over to death. This symbolic payment is to help ensure rebirth into a more affluent family.

The Soul After Death

Hindus do not fear death. It is another step in the soul's journey in the cycle of rebirth. Those who are truly enlightened at death achieve Maha Samadhi, "the Greatest Superconscious State" ("Death: Door to Immortality," 2). Some Hindu texts explain that the dying person sees divine light at the moment he or she expires. This light is an "illuminated consciousness" as the soul leaves the body. For those who are liberated from the cycle of rebirth, the soul is absorbed into Brahman, the great soul. Alternatively, depending on the person's beliefs, the soul may enter heaven to worship God for eternity.

Immediately after death, the soul remains near the family in their house. Many Hindus have reported seeing the person's spirit or being visited in dreams by their departed loved one. The 13-day period following death is an important time for the soul. Rituals performed during this time are meant to ensure that the person understands he or she has died, improve karmas to influence rebirth, and strengthen the new body the person will inhabit when he or she is reborn.

Observing death rituals is important for at least three reasons:

1. These customs assist the soul in whatever ways it needs.
2. The rituals honor the family's ancestors with whom the soul reunites.
3. These traditions improve the karma of those who perform them.

It is thus considered a sacred duty to carry out the many rituals involved in the 13-day mourning period and each year thereafter.

Initial Funeral Customs

In keeping with supporting the soul's journey to and through the afterlife, several rituals are performed. The timing of these observances is either before the sun sets on the day of death or within 24 hours.

A chief mourner is designated and is responsible for ensuring that rituals are properly performed. The chief mourner often is the deceased's eldest son. Others within the family's lineage may be chosen when necessary. At the funeral, mourners may dress casually. White is the preferred color for both males and females. Black is inappropriate, as is fancy clothing.

With few exceptions, most Hindus are cremated. This practice is consistent with the belief in reincarnation. Cremating the body helps the soul leave this life and move on in the cycle of rebirth. To prepare for cremation, the chief mourner and other relatives of the deceased's gender bathe the body in Ganges water, adorn it with ritual markings, and dress it in new clothes dipped in water from the Ganges. The thumbs and big toes are tied together to prevent the arms and legs from separating and to prevent the spirit from escaping. Widows put wedding pendants around husbands' necks, signifying enduring bonds.

After preparations, the body remains in the house until taken to the crematorium. The floor is cleaned where the body is placed. The body is draped with a white sheet with the head exposed. A lamp is lit at the person's head and stays lit throughout the 13-day mourning period. This light guides the soul's journey through the afterlife. A pot of water remains next to the lamp, which is refreshed daily to quench the soul's thirst.

Family, friends, and neighbors visit steadily during the first 24 hours to support mourners and pay last respects. Children are not shielded from death. It is considered a natural part of life and a sacred experience, as the soul continues its spiritual journey.

Mourners sit near the body, chant hymns, and pray for the deceased's soul. They walk around the body in a circle to create two barriers. One is meant to protect the deceased from evil spirits. The other helps ease the separation between the family and their lost loved one.

A ritual extending from the first day through the 13-day mourning period is the pinda ceremony. A pinda is a ball of rice that feeds the soul symbolically. The first pinda is placed where the person died. Others are set along the crematorium route and on the funeral pyre platform. Pindas are offered daily next to the lamp and the pot of water. They nourish the soul and strengthen the new body in which the spirit will be reborn. Pindas also protect the soul from evil spirits.

Before cremation, the family either builds a special fire shelter (homa) or starts a fire in the home. A fire ceremony is held to bless one brass pot and one clay pot. These vessels are brought to the cremation ceremony. The family constructs the casket that will carry the body to the crematorium. A garland of seasonal flowers may adorn the body for its final journey. The women of the household do not attend the cremation. They may wail openly as the body is taken away for the last time. The deceased's sons and other men in the procession take turns carrying the body through the community. Participation in the procession is a sacred act. The family priest does not visit the home the day following death. He joins the family at the cremation, offering prayers and support.

At the cremation ceremony, the body is carried three times

around the pyre. It is then positioned on the pyre platform. The chief mourner brings the clay pot filled with water and a pot containing embers from the homa fire. He carries the fire pot around the pyre, sprinkling the body with water to ease cremation's pain and quench the soul's thirst.

With the clay water pot, the priest circles the pyre three times. At each turn a hole is made in the pot, releasing water. The water surrounding the pyre protects the spirit and directs the soul upward as it leaves the body. The chief mourner breaks the water pot and lights the pyre, using embers from the homa fire. Mourners chant and wail as the body is cremated.

There is variation in how the cremation ceremony is conducted, but the common belief is that breaking the pot represents the pyre's cracking of the deceased's skull. This is the action that liberates the soul from the body. Some adherents believe that mourners should wait to hear the skull crack on the funeral pyre, marking the soul's escape. Others believe that the soul departs with the dying person's last breath. Regardless of timing, the spirit's release and subsequent journey are major mourning milestones.

Above, and following page: **Cremation, Ganges River, Varanasi, India (2020).**

The Mourning Period

While the men attend the cremation ceremony, the women stay or return home to bathe themselves and clean the house. At the cremation site and again after returning to the house, the men bathe themselves.

The family is considered impure throughout the 13-day mourning period, particularly the first 10 days before the deceased's ashes are scattered. The family remains at home. Close relatives stay with the mourners throughout the grieving period and sometimes longer. The family's impure status prevents them from attending other religious ceremonies during the mourning period. Some Hindus refrain from attending any ceremonies for the year following a loved one's death.

A widow wipes the wedding marks (sindoor) from her forehead to signify her changed marital status. Widows are relieved of their normal duties during their grief. Female friends and relatives take on household chores. The eldest son's wife takes the lead in these responsibilities.

Everyone in the house sleeps on the floor to be closer to Mother

Earth. The family fasts for the first day until after the cremation. Many believe that the family should not cook during the mourning period, so friends bring food for the family. In other households, female family members prepare the daily meals, which are strictly vegetarian.

Meals are an important part of the mourning process. Because the soul remains in the house and requires nourishment to be ready for its spiritual journey, the water that is set aside for the soul is accompanied daily by food to satisfy its hunger. Food eaten by the mourners is stripped of its most flavorful ingredients—garlic and ginger—for seven days. Hindu mourners may follow a sattvic diet consisting of foods intended to bring clarity to the mind. Meat, heavy seasonings, and ghee (clarified butter) are eliminated from daily meals. Food may be more boring than usual but is meant to detoxify the body.

Families generally refrain from desserts unless the deceased lived a long life. If the deceased lived a long, rich life to be celebrated, loved ones may enjoy a treat called ladoo, sweets made from flour and ghee and enhanced with chopped nuts, raisins, and coconut.

The chief mourner consults a pandit or knowledgeable relative to organize daily prayers, hymns, and readings of holy texts. Community members pay their respects throughout the 13-day mourning period, especially during a formal public condolence gathering after cremation. It is a sacred duty for everyone who knew the deceased or her or his family to pay their formal respects.

Daily the women of the family and community gather to mourn. A professional mourner might be hired to facilitate the process. Expressing emotions is encouraged, especially early in the mourning period when the women talk and share stories. This ritual makes it easier to talk openly about the deceased. Easing grief is an important aspect of supporting the soul's journey in the afterlife. Because the soul lingers in the house and observes family members grieving, witnessing the family in sorrow for too long hinders the soul's willingness to move on to the next life (Laungani, 52).

After a few days, the chief mourner collects the ashes to scatter in a river, preferably the Ganges. This generally occurs on the

10th day after death and is performed by the family priest. He recites holy texts, leading mourners in prayers to assist the deceased's spiritual salvation. Another pinda is offered on this day. For families who did not set out pindas every day, all 10 pindas are offered after the ashes are scattered. In accordance with the deceased's wishes, a meal for the poor may be coordinated in his honor after the scattering of ashes.

The Soul's Rebirth

The mourning period is very important for the deceased and the family. A new body is being created for the soul to inhabit during the first 12 days following death. Daily rituals (shahadah) involving offerings of pindas and food nourish the body and support the soul's journey.

The ceremony on the 12th day is considered even more important than the cremation and scattering of ashes. This is when the soul takes on its new body in the cycle of rebirth. If the deceased lived a good life, he or she will be liberated from the cycle and absorbed into Brahman. Failing to perform this ceremony keeps the soul from leaving the house and proceeding on its spiritual journey. The shahadah ritual on the 12th day also is significant for mourners because the deceased's soul joins its father, grandfather, and great-grandfather as an ancestral spirit. This encourages the family to worship and remember the deceased on a regular basis.

The soul's rejoining the ancestors is symbolized by a ritual in which one large pinda is formed representing the deceased and three smaller pindas are formed representing the three ancestors. The large pinda is divided into three and combined with the smaller ones. As the soul departs the house, this custom elevates the surviving first son to be the new head of the family.

Brahmins, priests of the highest caste in Hindu society, are invited to the shahadah ritual on the 12th day. One symbolically represents the deceased. Gifts are presented to the Brahmins that are thought to be items the deceased will need, such as bedding and clothes. The final ritual is observed on day 13, the last day of the mourning period. It is a fire ceremony in which offerings are made to the gods and the ancestors, of which the deceased is now a part.

Continuing Comfort for the Family

Even after the 13-day mourning period, communication with ancestors is important to daily Hindu culture. One month after death, a key mourner organizes another shahadah ritual, making a meal of the deceased's favorite foods, honoring ancestors, and giving gifts to Brahmins.

Monthly shahadah rituals continue until the one-year anniversary of death and on every anniversary thereafter. It is customary to give gifts to Brahmins annually to arrange for prayers in the loved one's memory and to give to the poor or donate to charitable organizations. Some Hindus make a daily offering in recognition of their loved ones. Hindus also collectively honor their ancestors for approximately two weeks every fall during Pitru Paksha. This timing coincides with the harvest season. These rituals allow everyone to remember and thank their ancestors, especially their parents, for their love and support.

The customs Hindus observe before, at the time of, and after death help both the deceased and his family progress. The traditions assist the soul in making a smooth transition to the next life. Observing the rituals also improves the karma of those who participate in the process. Ensuring the traditions are performed properly is an important part of the proceedings.

Although Hindus grieve deeply for the loss of their loved ones, death ultimately is seen as part of life. Comfort is found in the concept of the immortal soul continuing to live on in other bodies until it reaches spiritual attainment. Relationships are maintained through regular ancestor commemorations. Annual rituals mark milestones and give meaning to the death while enabling mourners to move forward ("Death and Dying," 2007, 64).

Hindus are encouraged to reflect regularly on their own death.

This is especially true when a loved one dies. Because death can lead to reincarnation, it serves as a reminder to refocus on letting go of worldly desires and on the ultimate goal of achieving spiritual enlightenment. This is the path of liberation from the cycle of rebirth.

Those who are overcome with grief can read scriptures about death, meditate, or visit a cremation ground to remind them that death is both an end and a beginning. With discipline and concentration, Hindus can transcend death and make it the transitory step in their spiritual journey.

Epilogue

To know how to die is to know how to live.—Ancient Buddhist philosophy

It often is said that life is a journey. The writing of these pages has been one for me. Thank you, dear reader, for accompanying me on this adventure. To journey is to move, to grow, to process. The experience transforms what is taken in by the senses along the way. We may marvel at the mystery of our own transformation. Objects and events are absorbed. They are then incorporated into the mind, guiding our constant voyaging into unknown territory.

Often, travelers do not know what they are seeking until they have found it. This is reminiscent of T.S. Eliot's oft-quoted insight "And the end of all our exploring will be to arrive where we started and know the place for the first time." The voyager's goal in the end, whatever its symbolism may be, is not a place or a thing but rather the achievement of a new level of being.

Paupers and princes have made such journeys throughout folk tales, seeking to discover the secrets of their true being by gaining new wisdom and rising to new heights of consciousness. In China, for example, tao has been the way of enlightenment for centuries: the pilgrim's path and ultimate goal.

Life's great events are acknowledged as journeys: conception and birth, various passages into adulthood, work, marriage, procreation, maturity, old age. To acquire a new skill is to venture toward growth. Prayer is a journey, as is the composition of poetry or music. To fall in love is to experience stunning change. To cultivate that love over years is both a journey and a transformation.

It seems appropriate, given the persistence of such realizations by those in so many lands and eras, that dying also has been viewed throughout history as a process of journeying. Comprehending death as one in a series of natural though mysterious personal transformations is so common that it could be considered a definitive trait of the human race.

Exceptions exist. Entire societies get trapped periodically in a kind of gray space of confusion about the facts of death. This can happen when the state of scientific knowledge contradicts the larger body of experience on which a sense of truth is based. Western attitudes toward death and dying have suffered in the past from such confusion.

At almost any time, a tribe or group can be found tucked in the hills of a primitive land, where death is seen as an assault on human dignity. To the Juiraros, for example, a tribe dwelling on the eastern slopes of the Andes there is no "natural death." While they may consider death a separation of spirit from body, they cannot seem to comprehend the general relation of natural causes for this. Each death is unintelligible, unnatural, accidental. Every death is presumably a murder, eliciting great excitement accompanied by the beating of signal drums (Stoddard, 262).

In modern society, ambulance sirens and telephones serve as signal drums. Frightened and feeling defeated by death, people forget the ancient wisdom of their heritage, wisdom that is still being imparted through a new set of observations.

Navajo Indians, curiously, are one of the few cultural groups on the globe to have taken the position that there is no life whatever after death. Individuals have always advanced notions along these lines. Societies as a whole have believed otherwise. Handed down to succeeding generations has been the idea that something leaves the body at the moment of death and perhaps enters another form or level of existence. The Navajo groups who denied this found it difficult to deal with the consequences of their denial. Their management of death and dying remains different from mainstream society even in conventional medical situations today.

The seriously ill Navajo was carried away from his hogan dwelling and isolated from all but one or two members of the tribe. These caregivers stayed and waited in dread for their sick friend to die.

Silence was standard when death arrived. No mourning or mention of death was considered appropriate. Quickly, the body and all the deceased's personal belongings were burned. This included the hogan. The ashes were buried out of sight.

So powerful was the denial of death in these groups that the person who had stayed with the dying and performed the final rites was shunned afterward as taboo. It was believed that death was the end. It was too terrible an event to be allowed into tribal existence. Yet, death is obviously not the end. Death itself in such a society must be confronted in a ritualized attempt to kill it. It is life that dies, while death lives on.

Our own defense mechanisms represent the same ritualistic defeat of conscious purpose. Still, we have a choice. We can dare a new perspective, and in so doing we can change. In the face of death, we can decide to remain open, not to withdraw in dismay from the dying individual, not to shun the bereaved. We can opt not to resist the realities of the mourning process.

If we care to trust humanity's accumulated wisdom on the subject and informed belief about it, we can stay open to the experience of our own dying. We can do so with the feeling that it will be in some way a familiar journey, akin to the journey of being born. A readiness to depart their earthly existence has been the attitude of the wise, the elderly, and the religious throughout history. That same sense has been reflected by the mystics, prophets, and poets of every era. This holds true as well for countless millions of ordinary, practical people who have stood watch at the deathbeds of loved ones, who have held the dying in their arms, gazing straight into their eyes, listening to their last words, and closely observing what was transpiring. The dying didn't resist. They prepared themselves quietly and in a timely manner for a peaceful departure.

From centuries of experience comes the conclusion that death appears to be a process rather than an event. It seems to be a passage for human life that in some way continues to exist and journey on. Rituals meant to respond to this view are themselves life-enhancing. Among common people such customs are as realistic and practical as their care has been for the dying.

In Eastern European villages, for example, doors and windows traditionally have been opened widely immediately after the death of an occupant so the spirit could move unrestricted into the life beyond. For similar purpose, holes were drilled into the rooftops of houses in rural Mexico. Ashanti tribes in Ghana have a tradition of providing water until the dying's last breath. This is to make it easier for the thirsting spirit to climb the steep hill to eternity. A handkerchief also is placed in the hands of the deceased to wipe away the sweat of the struggle into the next world. Villagers in Moslem Turkey leave a light burning for 40 days and nights after a death, believing that the newly released soul may need help learning to live without a physical body. Japanese Buddhists in country villages sew a white pilgrim's garment for the body and place a bag of coins at its belt so the departing spirit can pay the boatman for passage into eternity.

Death as liberation is a familiar motif throughout the world's cultures. In India, the shahadah ceremony is performed by Hindus to assist the spiritual body to its celestial abode. Death is viewed as the moment of freedom when the final journey begins. The Korean *cho-hon* ceremony is an "invitation to the soul" during this stage of transition. *Sajas* are the messengers who come to guide the soul on its pilgrimage. Viking chieftains who died were sent to sea in their ships with all their belongings on board for the voyage to the afterlife. The vessels were set ablaze to free the spirit from its material bonds.

These are universal responses to the mysterious transitional process of human life that have been observed throughout the ages by people of wholly contrasting cultures and are essentially the same. Death is a passage toward the liberation that exists beyond space and time. Biological death can be understood as the obliteration of the final barriers between an individual and his or her God. Death may be seen as the ultimate achievement of transcendence.

Often, rites for this final passage are performed as caregivers observe religious disciplines such as fasting, meditating, and praying. There is a realization that transformation cannot happen without a letting go of ego, a small death of its own. A judgment appears in various forms in such ancient works as the Egyptian *Book of the*

Dead, the Tibetan *Bardo Thodol*, and the medieval Christian work *The Craft of Dying* (*Ars Moriendi*).

There is general agreement that the state of mind of the dying individual is of utmost importance to her or his eventual destiny. Death is perceived as a sort of journey. The description of the process in the "secret" Tibetan book is extremely complicated but fascinating in its similarity to the descriptions of modern subjects who describe near-death experiences. Tibetans teach that the dying person at the moment life ceases will see a brilliant light. The person will go through a series of struggles that represent different levels of spiritual development under attack from tempting forces of worldly negativity. Escape from the nearly inevitable fate of reincarnation can only be attained by resisting all of life's illusions and entering at last into the ecstatic state of Samadhi, the Clear Light of the Void.

The esoteric *Bardo Thodol* is like an instruction booklet for the newly deceased. It is to be recited by the dying individual's spiritual guide for many days so that, in all the confusion at life's end, its wisdom will not be missed. Medieval Christians in *Ars Moriendi*, not believing in reincarnation, felt that such spiritual counseling must occur as the person was expiring. This approach emphasized the confession of sins and the death of egoistic desires before the person should come into the presence of God. Both the Tibetan and Christian ways advanced the ancient Buddhist philosophy "to know how to die is to know how to live." Both believed that these spiritual teachings should be part of daily life for all who sought enlightenment.

Most of the world's major religions concur that the manner of death is significant. They also agree that the care of the dying is a delicate matter best handled by the yogi, the priest, or a congregational elder with great powers of spiritual authority. Right dying, according to Tibetan sages, is an initiation. This process should occur consciously. The ultimate goal of union with the divine, however defined, is the same for most religions. That East and West have tended to disagree on how long this takes and where it takes place is relatively insignificant in light of the fact that both perspectives aim to assist the individual out of time and space and into eternity.

238

Epilogue

"Early or late, all must answer the summons to return to the Reservoir of Being. For we lose our hold on life when our time has come, as the leaf falls from the bough when its day is done. The deeds of the righteous enrich the world, as the fallen leaf enriches the soil beneath."— *Gates of Prayer: The New Union Prayerbook* (New York: CCAR, 1975)

Bibliography

Adichie, C.N. *Notes on Grief.* New York: Knopf, 2021.

Albom, Mitch. *Tuesdays with Morrie.* New York: Broadway Books, 1997.

Alter, Cathy. "'Pandemic Grief' Proves Especially Devastating and Complex for Many in Mourning, Health Experts Say." *Washington Post,* March 28, 2021.

American Psychiatric Association. *Diagnostic and Statistical Manual of Mental Disorders,* Fifth Edition, Text Revision (DSM-5-TR). Washington, D.C.: American Psychiatric Association, 2022.

Archer, John. *The Nature of Grief: The Evolution and Psychology of Reactions to Loss.* London: Routledge, 1999.

Arrien, Angeles. *The Second Half of Life: Opening the Eight Gates of Wisdom.* Boulder: Sounds True, 2005.

Attig, Thomas. "Meanings of Death Seen through the Lens of Grieving." *Death Studies* 28, no. 4 (2004): 341–60.

Attwood, Bain. *Telling the Truth About Aboriginal History.* Sydney: Southwood Press, 2005.

Barnes, Julian. *Levels of Life.* New York: Knopf, 2013.

Becker, Carl. "Aging, Dying, and Bereavement in Contemporary Japan." *Frontiers of Japanese Philosophy 4: Facing the 21st Century.* Nagoya: Nanzan Institute for Religion & Culture, 2009.

Bengston, Vern, Norella M. Putney, Merril Silverstein, and Susan C. Harris. "Does Religiosity Increase with Age?" *Journal for the Scientific Study of Religion* 54, no. 2 (2015): 363–79.

Berachot. First Tractate of Seder Zeraim ("Order of Seeds") of the Mishna and of the Talmud. https://www.sefaria.org/Jerusalem_Talmud_Berakhot?tab=contents.

Bolitho, Harold. *Bereavement and Consolation: Testimonials from Tokugawa, Japan.* New Haven: Yale University Press, 2003.

Bourassa, Kyle, Lindsey Knowles, David Sbarra, and Mary-Francis O'Connor. "Absent but Not Gone: Interdependence in Couples' Quality of Life Persists After a Partner's Death." *Psychological Science* 27, no. 2 (2016): 270–81.

Brahmaprana, Pravrajika. "Vedanta: Death and the Art of Dying." *Cross Currents* 51, no. 3 (2001): 337–46.

Brinkmann, Svend. *Grief: The Price of Love.* Cambridge: Polity, 2020.

Brody, Jane. "Recovery Varies After a Spouse Dies." *New York Times,* September 27, 2016.

Bruce, L.L., and T.J. Leary. "The Limbic System of Tetrapods: A Comparative Analysis of Cortical and Amygdalar Populations." *Brain Behavior Evolution* 46, nos. 4–5 (1995): 224–34.

Caruso, Lynn. "Partingway Blessing for a Pet." In *Grieving with Your Whole Heart,* 116–17. Introduction by Thomas Moore. Woodstock, VT: SkyLight Paths, 2015.

Coleman, Peter G., and Marie A. Mills. "Uncertain Faith Later in Life: Studies of the Last Religious Generation in England." In *New Dimensions in Spirituality, Religion, and Aging,* eds. Vern L. Bengtson and Merril Silverstein, 86–112. Routledge, 2019.

Bibliography

Cragun, Ryan T., Christel Manning, and Lori L. Fazzino, eds. *Organized Secularism in the United States: New Directions in Research*. Berlin: de Gruyter, 2017.

"Death and Dying." *Hinduism Today*, January 1, 1997.

"Death and Dying." *Hinduism Today*, January 1, 2007.

Devine, Megan. *It's OK That You're Not OK*. Boulder: Sounds True, 2017.

Diamant, Anita. *Saying Kaddish: How to Comfort the Dying, Bury the Dead, and Mourn as a Jew*. New York: Schocken, 1999.

Didion, Joan. *The Year of Magical Thinking*. New York: Vintage, 2007.

Dodge, Christine H. *The Everything Understanding Islam Book*. Avon, MA: F+A Publications, 2003.

Doka, Kenneth J. *Grief Is a Journey: Finding Your Path through Loss*. New York: Atria Books, 2016.

Ecklund, E.H., and K.S. Lee. "Atheists Negotiate Religion and Family." *Journal for the Scientific Study of Religion* 50, no. 4 (2011): 728–43.

Edgell, Penny, Douglas Hartmann, Evan Stewart, and Joseph Gerteis. "Atheists and Other Cultural Outsiders: Moral Boundaries and the Non-Religious in the United States." *Social Forces* 95, no. 2 (2016): 607–38.

Editors of *Hinduism Today* Magazine. *What Is Hinduism? Modern Adventures into a Profound Global Faith*. Kapaa, HI: Himalayan Academy, 2007.

"Every 28 Seconds." *Washington Post*, February 21, 2021.

Firth, Shirley. *Dying, Death and Bereavement in a British Hindi Community*. Leuven: Peeters, 1997.

Fuchs, Thomas. "Presence in Absence: The Ambiguous Phenomenology of Grief." *Phenomenology and the Cognitive Sciences* 17 (2018): 195–98.

Gay, Peter. *Freud: A Life for Our Time*. New York: Norton, 1988.

Glaskin, Katie, Myrna Tonkinson, Yasmine Musharbash, and Victoria Burban. *Mortality, Mourning and Mortuary Practices in Indigenous Australia*. Surrey: Ashgate, 2008.

Gockel, Annemarie. "Telling the Ultimate Tale: The Merits of Narrative Research in the Psychology of Religion." *Qualitative Research in Psychology* 10 (2013): 189–203.

Granek, Leeat. "Disciplinary Wounds: Has Grief Become the Identified Patient for a Field Gone Awry?" *Journal of Loss and Trauma* 18, no. 3 (2013): 275–83.

Greenwood, Faine. "Japanese Emperor Will Break Burial Tradition by Being Cremated." Public Radio International, November 15, 2013.

Gupta, Rashmi. "Death Beliefs and Practices from an Asian Indian American Hindu Perspective." *Death Studies* 35, no. 3 (2011): 244–66.

Halevi, Leor. "Wailing for the Dead: The Role of Women in Early Islamic Funerals." *Past & Present* 183, no. 1 (2004): 3–40.

Heywood, Bethany T., and Jesse M. Bering. "Meant to Be: How Religious Beliefs and Cultural Religiosity Affect the Implicit Bias to Think Teleologically." *Religion, Brain and Behavior* 4, no. 3 (2013): 183–201.

Hirai, Atsuko. *Government by Mourning: Death and Political Integration in Japan, 1603–1912*. Cambridge: Harvard University Press, 2014.

Holinger, Dorothy P. *The Anatomy of Grief*. New Haven: Yale University Press, 2020.

Holmes, Thomas, and R. Rahe. "The Holmes-Rahe Life Stress Inventory." Adapted from "Holmes-Rahe Social Adjustment Rating Scale." *Journal of Psychosomatic Research* 2 (1967): 1–76.

"How Enlightened Beings Die: Ten Stories of the Final Moments of Great Sages & Ten Reasons Hindus Do Not Fear Death." *Hinduism Today*, July 1, 2018.

Hwang, Karen, Joseph H. Hammer, and Ryan T. Cragun. "Extending Religion-Health Research to Secular Minorities: Issues and Concerns." *Journal of Religion and Health* 50 (2011): 608–22.

Islamic Relief UK. "Five Pilars of Islam." https://www.islamic-relief.org.uk/resources/knowledge-base/five-pillars-of-islam/.

Bibliography

Jacklin, M. "Collaboration and Closure: Negotiating Indigenous Mourning Protocols in Australian Life Writing." *Antipodes* 19, no. 2 (2005): 184–91.

Jeffreys, J. Shep. *Helping Grieving People—When Tears Are Not Enough: A Handbook for Care Providers*, 2nd ed. New York: Routledge/Taylor and Francis, 2011.

Jonker, Gerdien. "The Many Facets of Islam: Death, Dying and Disposal Between Orthodox Rule and Historic Convention." In *Death and Bereavement Across Cultures*, eds. C.M. Parkes, P. Laungani, and W. Young, 47–165. London: Routledge, 1997.

Katz, Jack. *How Emotions Work*. Chicago: University of Chicago Press, 1999.

Khadro, Sangye. *Preparing for Death and Helping the Dying: A Buddhist Perspective*. Singapore: Kong Meng San Phor Kark See Monastery, 1999.

Kilmartin, Laurie. *Dead People Suck: A Guide for Survivors of the Newly Departed*. New York: Rodale, 2017.

Kübler-Ross, Elisabeth. *On Death & Dying*. New York: Scribner, 1967.

Laungani, Pittu. "Death in a Hindu Family." In *Death and Bereavement Across Cultures*, eds. C.M. Parkes, P. Laungani, and W. Young, 52–72. London: Routledge, 1997.

Lee, Sherman A., and Robert Neimeyer. "Pandemic Grief Scale: A Screening Tool for Dysfunctional Grief Due to Covid-19 Loss." *Death Studies* 46, no. 1 (2022): 14–24.

Lewis, Clive Staple. *A Grief Observed*. New York: Harper One, 1994.

Magowan, Fiona. *Melodies of Mourning: Music and Emotion in Northern Australia*. Oxford: James Currey, 2007.

Mandell, Sherri. *The Blessing of a Broken Heart*. London: Toby, 2009.

Manning, Christel. "Facing Death Without Religion: Secular Sources Like Science Work Well for Meaning Making." *Harvard Divinity Bulletin*, Autumn/Winter 2019.

Manning, Christel. "Meaning Making Narratives Among Non-Religious Individuals Facing the End of Life." In *New Dimensions in Spirituality, Religion, and Aging*, eds. Vern Bengston and Merril Silverstein, 1–26. London: Routledge 2019.

Martin, Alexander. "Modern Mourning at Japan's High-Tech Cemeteries." *Nikkei Asian Review*, July 5, 2017.

Merleau-Ponty, Maurice. *Phenomenology of Perception*. London: Routledge, 2012.

Miller, Mark. "Complicated Grief Late in Life." *National Library of Medicine* 14, no. 2 (June 2012).

Moore, Melinda, and Daniel A. Roberts. *The Suicide Funeral: Honoring Their Memory, Comforting Their Survivors.* Wipf and Stock Publishers, 2017.

Nakata, Hiroko. "Japan's Funerals Deep-Rooted Mix of Ritual, Form." *Japan Times*, July 28, 2009.

Neimeyer, Robert A., and Sherman A. Lee. "Circumstances of the Death and Associated Risk Factors for Severity and Impairment of Covid-19 Grief." National Center for Biotechnology Information, National Library of Medicine, May 21, 2021.

Nhat Hanh, Thich. *Breathe, You Are Alive: The Sutra of the Full Awareness of Breathing.* Berkeley: Parallax, 2008.

O'Hara, Delia. "Paul Slovic Observes the 'Psychic Numbing' of Covid-19." American Psychological Association, November 30, 2020.

Ortega, Robert M., and Kathleen C. Faller. "Training Child Welfare Workers from an Intersectional Cultural Humility Perspective: A Paradigm Shift." *Child Welfare* 90, no. 5 (2011): 27–49.

Parkes, Colin Murray, Pittu Laungani, and William Young. Introduction. In *Death and Bereavement across Cultures*, 2nd ed., eds. C.M. Parkes, P. Laungani, and B. Young. London: Routledge, 2015.

Perez, Ai Faithy. "The Complicated Rituals of Japanese Funerals." *Savvy Tokyo*, October 21, 2015.

Phillips, Adam. *Becoming Freud: The Making of a Psychoanalyst*. New Haven: Yale University Press, 2014.

Pulvers, Roger. "Dealing with Death the Japanese Ways." *Japan Times*, November 26, 2006.

Bibliography

Rahman, Jamal. "Not All Tears Are Equal." In *Grieving with Your Whole Heart*, 40–42, Introduction by Thomas Moore. Woodstock, VT: SkyLight Paths, 2015.

Rando, Therese A. *Treatment of Complicated Mourning*. Champaign, IL: Research Press, 1993.

Rinpoche, Sogyal. *The Tibetan Book of Living and Dying*. San Francisco: HarperCollins, 1993.

Rosenblatt, Roger. *Kayak Morning: Reflections on Love, Grief and Small Boats*. New York: Ecco, 2012.

Rosenblatt, Roger. *Making Toast*. New York: HarperCollins, 2010.

Ross, H.M. "Islamic Tradition at the End of Life." *Medical-Surgical Nursing* 10, no. 2 (2001): 83–87.

Senju, A. *Gozen-no-Okuribi* (Part 1). The Kyoto Project, 2008.

Serres, Michel. *Statues: The Second Book of Foundations*. London: Bloomsbury, 2015.

Smith, A.H. "The Culture of Kabira, Southern Ryukyu Islands." *Proceedings of the American Philosophical Society* 104 (1960): 134–71.

Solomon, Sheldon, Jeff Greenberg, and Tom Pyszcynski. *The Worm at the Core: On the Role of Death in Life*. New York: Random House, 2015.

Stearns, Peter N. *Revolutions in Sorrow: The American Experience of Death in Global Perspective*. Boulder: Paradigm, 2007.

Stoddard, Sandoval. *The Hospice Movement*. New York: Vintage, 1978.

Suhail, K. Jamil, J.R. Oyebode, and Asir Ajmal. "Continuing Bonds in Bereaved Pakistani Muslims: Effects of Culture and Religion." *Death Studies* 35, no. 1 (2011): 22–41.

Sun, Anna. "Turning Ghosts into Ancestors in Contemporary China." *Harvard Divinity Bulletin*, Spring/Summer 2019.

Van der Kolk, Bessel. *The Body Keeps the Score*. New York: Viking, 2014.

Venbrux, Eric. *A Death in the Tiwi Islands: Conflict, Ritual and Social Life in an Australian Aboriginal Community*. Cambridge: Cambridge University Press, 1995.

Verdery, Ashton M., Emily Smith-Greenaway, Rachel Margolis, and Jonathan Daw. "Tracking the Reach of Covid-19 Kin Loss with a Bereavement Multiplier to the U.S." *Proceedings of the National Academy of Sciences*, July 10, 2020.

Webb, Gisela. "When Death Occurs: Islamic Rituals and Practices in the U.S." In *Religion, Death, and Dying*, Vol. 3, *Bereavement and Death Rituals*, ed. L. Bregman, 111–26. Santa Barbara, CA: Praeger, 2010.

Weber, Samuel, Kenneth Pargament, and Mark E. Kunik. "Psychological Distress Among Religious Nonbelievers: A Systematic Review." *Journal of Religion and Health* 51, no. 1 (2012): 72–86.

Wei-Ming, Tu. *Confucian Thought: Selfhood as Creative Transformation*. Albany: SUNY Press, 1985.

Wei-Ming, Tu, and Mary Evelyn Tucker. *Confucian Spirituality*, Vol. 2. Chestnut Ridge, NY: Herder & Herder, 2004.

Wilkinson, P.J., and Peter G. Coleman. "Strong Beliefs and Coping in Old Age: A Case-Based Comparison of Atheism and Religious Faith." *Ageing and Society* 30, no. 2 (2010): 337–61.

Winnicott, D.W. *Home Is Where We Start From*. New York: Norton, 1990.

Wiren, Alan. "Japanese Funerals Rites." Japan Experience, December 25, 2012.

Wong, Eva. *Taoism: An Essential Guide*. Boston: Shambhala, 2011.

Worden, J. William. *Grief Counseling and Grief Therapy*. New York: Springer, 2018.

Wozniak, Barbara. "Religiousness, Well-Being and Ageing: Selected Explanations of Positive Relationships." *Anthropological Review* 78, no. 3 (2015): 259–68.

Yasien-Esmael, Hend, and Simon Shimshon Rubin. "The Meaning Structures of Muslim Bereavements in Israel: Religious Traditions, Mourning Practices, and Human Experience." *Death Studies* 29, no. 6 (2005): 495–518.

Zepp, Ira G. *A Muslim Primer*. Fayetteville: University of Arkansas Press, 2000.

Zola, Luigi. *The Father: Historical, Psychological and Cultural Perspectives*, rev. ed. Trans. Henry Martin. London: Routledge, 2018.

Index

245

Index